THE PREDATOR

THE ART AND MAKING OF THE FILM

THE PREDATOR:
THE ART AND MAKING OF THE FILM

ISBN: 9781785657016

Published by Titan Books
A division of Titan Publishing Group Ltd.
144 Southwark St.
London
SE1 0UP

First edition: September 2018
10 9 8 7 6 5 4 3 2 1

To receive advance information, news, competitions, and exclusive offers online,
please sign up for the Titan newsletter on our website: www.titanbooks.com

Did you enjoy this book? We love to hear from our readers.
Please e-mail us at: readerfeedback@titanemail.com or write to Reader
Feedback at the above address.

A CIP catalogue record for this title is available from the British Library.
Printed and bound in the United States.

ABOUT THE AUTHOR
A London-based writer, **James Nolan**'s essays and articles have appeared in numerous
publications, including *1001 Movies You Must See Before You Die, 1001 Comics You Must Read
Before You Die* and *The Greatest Movies You'll Never See.*

THE PREDATOR

THE ART AND MAKING OF THE FILM

JAMES NOLAN

TITAN BOOKS

CONTENTS

Before filming commenced on *The Predator*, Shane Black sent the following 'mission statement' to the principal cast members in order to explain his vision for the film...

THE PREDATOR - MISSION STATEMENT BY SHANE BLACK

As we contemplate the fourth installment, and (unbelievably} the 30th year in which this fucking alien rears his head, a brief note.

Okay, not that brief. I like to choke people with paper. Memos, thoughts... all by way of getting us on the same page. I'll let you into my process and, in turn, invite whatever you're willing to share. The goal? Commonality. A mission statement, prior to production.

Let's get to it.

For starters, in one of those odd unintended coincidences, the movie's plot is about 'updating' the current model; using recombinant DNA to evolve a better, latter-day take on the classic *Predator*. Which, not coincidentally, is exactly the alchemy we're attempting. And no better place to start, I think, than a conversation about hybrids.

THE MOVIE IS A HYBRID

If this were entirely a horror film, we'd have a much easier go of it; that's a traveled path, plenty of signage. Likewise, if it were just an action movie, we'd strut our melancholy, macho selves into the gunfire, and call it a day.

We're doing both.

The first *Predator* film (circa 1987) offers as good a template as any. It's unmistakably a hybrid, combining the 1980's *Alien/Terminator* craze and the *Commando/First Blood* craze. Turns out it's also a lot of folks' favorite film; this, despite being closer to John Carpenter's *The Thing*, perhaps, than to *Jurassic World*.

On the one hand, it's a lark. Everyone loves the tough-guy zingers, for instance ("I ain't got time to bleed...") Yet, another look at that film reveals a somber, surprisingly nihilistic side. The characters are sweating and afraid; their tormenter is rarely seen, merely glimpsed. And, of course, they all fucking die—save, of course, for a shell-shocked, possibly insane Schwarzenegger.

Humor and despair. Heroism amidst futility. Mounting dread, mixed with just the slightest wink to the audience (it being Schwarzenegger, after all). It's a seldom seen combination, which in its purest form brought us *Butch Cassidy and the Sundance Kid*. And, to that point...

THE BECKONING

The surest way to stay on top, I believe, is to remember to touch bottom; to find what's *mythic* here. To that end, 30 years of marinating in the zeitgeist only helps us. Previous *Predator* sequels exist; see them, enjoy them—and know we're aiming higher.

A brief word, if you will, about myth: there's the story of a man out for a Sunday drive with his family, who, upon seeing a man dangling helplessly from a nearby cliff, promptly slams on his brakes, leaps from the car, leaves behind his wife and two children, and dashes to the rescue. He climbs down, clutching bits of brush, pulls the helpless man to safety. Nearly kills BOTH of them.

Joseph Campbell comments on this situation: why, with his own family to think of, would a man risk near death to protect a random stranger, leaving his own kids fatherless? Possibly, says Campbell, because myth trumps logic and even self-preservation. Our Sunday driver didn't know it, but he was looking at an UNFINISHED MYTH: a perilous situation, old as time, with a missing element—a hole, if you will, in the pattern.

The driver's new job, instantly acquired, was to complete the picture by providing RESCUER to the tapestry. His brain saw a missing piece; the need to complete the myth was compelling, unavoidable. It wakes up in us this desire to fulfill the narrative that we all know, deep inside. To recognize, amidst everyday blah, the undeniable moments when we STEP INTO A STORY; one with rules and obligations. The shadow of who we CAN be beckons.

(Ha! Two pages in, and the bullshit's flowing. NICE.)

The broken soldiers in our story are unignited flares. Dud grenades, overlooked... but still dangerous. Myths-in-training, looking for a kick-start.

THIS IS A WESTERN

Myth embodied imperfectly; in cracked, simple vessels. Knights in tarnished armor. This is our landscape, I think.

Concerning the Western: Interesting fact (to me): American fiction boasts two specific protagonists indigenous to our great country: namely, the cowboy and the private eye. Until relatively recently, there was no 'Westerns' shelf in Dutch bookstores (although they did beat us to porn) and similarly, the tough detective—popularized by Hammett, honed by Chandler and perfected by Ross Macdonald—is likewise an American creation. A consequence of our cowboy past. It's no coincidence that the same authors who penned the first hardboiled P.I. stories in the 30's alternately pumped out Westerns to equally rabid demand.

The interesting thing (to me) is how the P.I. genre started with streetwise, world-weary pragmatists. A no-nonsense 'kind of red-tape-cutting' justice.

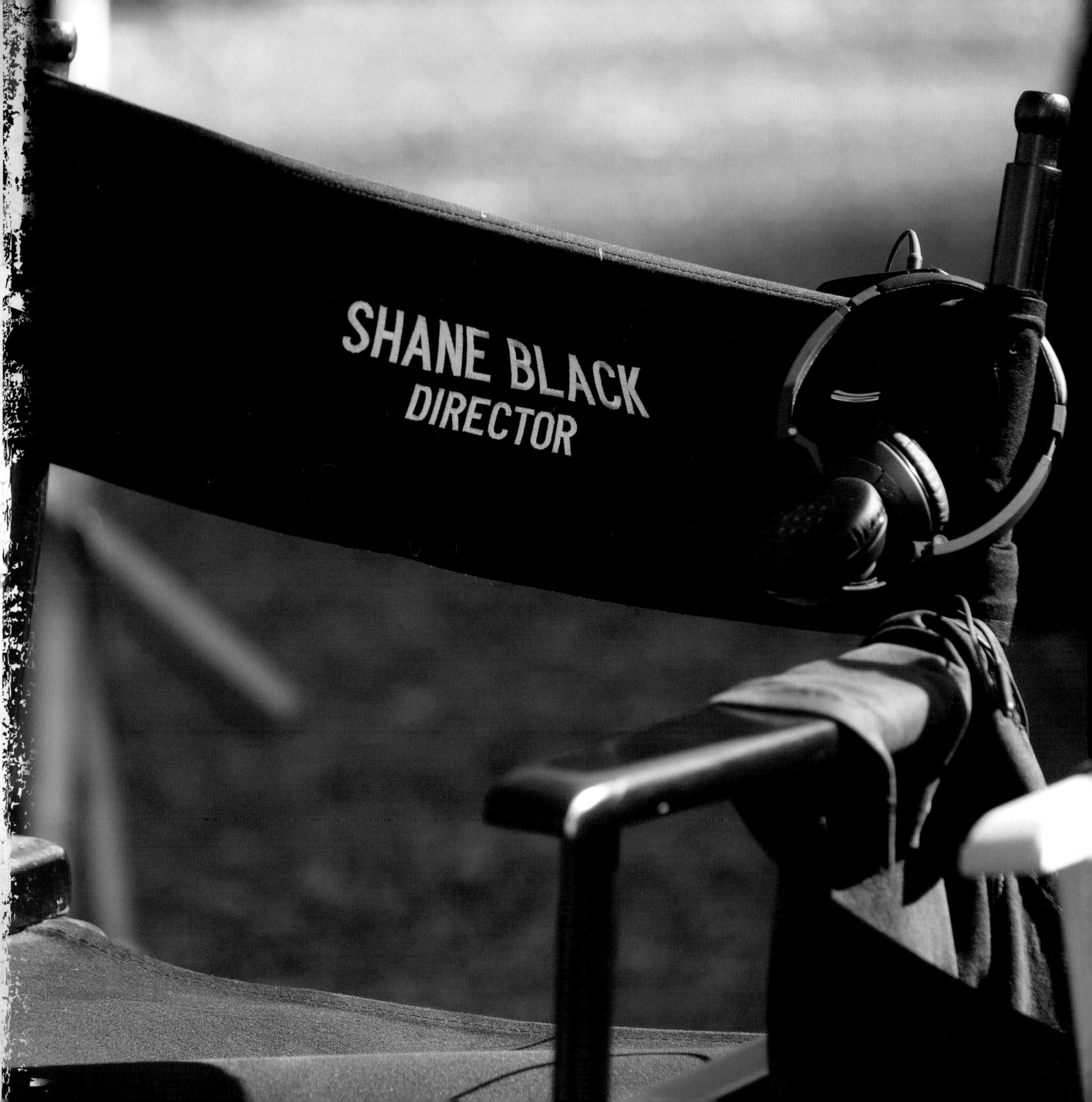
SHANE BLACK
DIRECTOR

AND THEN, SOMETHING ELSE BECAME APPARENT: These same no-nonsense heroes became the perfect venue for *existential themes and stories*. Sometimes the best way, it seemed, to tell an existential story was to assign it not to a philosopher/protagonist but rather to a JOE, a regular guy, who believes in the value of being *unimaginative*.

LOVELY. NO COWBOY BOOKS IN DUTCH. WHAT'S YOUR POINT?

I'm getting there. Put a different way: poor writing often consists of stating a simple thought in unnecessarily flowery and convoluted language. Conversely, good writing often occurs when a character of few words, of limited vocabulary, must struggle to express a complex idea; a vaguely glimpsed bit of existential insight.

Our characters fall into this latter category. Gunslingers will once again walk this landscape. They just don't know they're gunslingers. They may not even realize they have a creed.

YOU OKAY THAT THE HEROES ARE ALL HEAD CASES?

I got no problem with that, so long as it doesn't interfere with their being cool.

AND BY 'COOL', I ASSUME YOU MEAN THAT MANIC, SLIGHTLY WARPED YET EFFORTLESSLY SLICK BUTTON-DOWN MACHO STYLE, ENDEMIC TO THE 70'S?

Sure. Whatever you say. The MEN in this movie are going to be great. The loose-limbed, rumpled charm of them.

I SEE. YOU DO KNOW THERE'S A WOMAN ON THE TEAM TOO?

No, I fucking forgot... Of course I know! Same knighthood, different sex. This movie is about evolving, about *becoming*. Last I looked, that's not gender-specific. The men and women exhibit a common trait: they scratch their head at the world they inhabit. They're an imperfect fit.

I BELIEVE THE WORD IS 'MISFIT'.

Yes, it is. Are you going to keep being an asshole?

YES. I BELIEVE SO.

Fine, whatever. To wit: the first misfit I ever conceived on film was the character played by Mel Gibson in *Lethal Weapon*. I wrote it as a Frankenstein story, if that makes sense.

PRECIOUS LITTLE.

Fine, I'll spell it out, walk you through my thinking back then.

OBOY. HERE WE GO...

You got a guy, in Vietnam he's a gunslinger. Now, back home, he's out of his element, sitting in a Denny's surrounded by complacent, whining families... people who feel shrouded, safe.

He's seen and done things no one can feasibly bear—and he's a monster to his neighbors. A freak. A rusty, violent dinosaur in an age when the gunslingers are fading. Dodge City is gentrified. They think the gunslinger's time is past. They can afford to. They spit on our Frankenstein, they call him babykiller.

Except our Frankenstein knows a secret: violence never sleeps. All the PTA meetings in the world won't convince him the war's over. It just goes in waves.

So he watches bad TV, and drinks. It's easy, and it doesn't distract him. He toasts the ten dead guys who deserve his medal more than him. Comes to find Dodge City's civilized veneer is just that; thin, illusory. Sure enough, violence *notices* the soft suburbs...

BOOM. Now, the citizens are hit and bleeding, and they all come to Frankenstein's cage and say, "Hey, we were wrong—we reviled you, called you a monster, but now we NEED you. You see, you know all the things we've forgotten."

In a pinch, they always default to the Frankenstein... who knew all along. Our faded gunslinger. A misfit with a skill-set. He can subvert it, throttle it, upend a truckload of Scotch in a frantic attempt to drown it... and yet it lingers. His armor is old, ugly, and rusted, but armor it is, in the final analysis. Knights have that.

The misfit as hero is the difference that I hope we can bring to our new, updated entry in the *Predator* saga.

THE TEAM

The biggest divergence, perhaps, from previous *Predator* movies lies in our choice of soldiers; the 'greener, leaner, misdemeanor' version, so to speak, of Arnold's crack anti-terror squad from 1987. They've been counted out, to a man, by the established order. Marginalized and mothballed. It's unclear whether some have committed crimes (although, that said, it's important that we not portray them as criminals—this is not a prison bus they're on).

The first *Predator* script offered little or no clue, going into production, as to any distinction between characters, beyond the weapons they carried (or, in my case, the glasses they wore). Their initial dialogue was all but interchangeable and usually involved the word 'Foxtrot'. It is my goal to cast a noir net over the whole wriggling bunch of you, and, with your help, embrace the notion of elevating this material.

The goal? To offer up entirely unlikely heroes. The least qualified bunch, in many ways, to undertake a task even the army and CIA are ill-equipped to handle.

I've always found beginning a story (that mocking blank page) to be altogether frightening. What I do is all I know to do: I continue to type until I am distracted by something which, for that brief second, is momentarily of more interest than my own fear. Sometimes, all that's required is a glance at the taped message above my desk, which reads simply: "Schmuck—this is important".

Fear and purpose can't live in the same room; in that vein, it will be fun to find the instances where our broken soldiers are snapped out of dissonance; the moments in which (albeit briefly) the spit-in-the-wind grin emerges to trump fear; in which implicit knowledge trumps uncertainty. In which they remember they're gunslingers.

A WORD ON ACTION CLICHÉS...

And what we make of them. Me, I'd lobby for standing them on their head whenever the chance presents itself (you can't do it all the time, of course, or it becomes predictable; itself a cliché).

Example. There's an oft-repeated beat in tough-guy movies, usually during an interrogation scene: the bad guy is slumped in a chair, sullen. He won't talk. So our lead says, "Memory not so good, huh? How about now?" He puts a *single bullet* in the chamber of a six-shooter, points it and—*click*—!

The bad guy freaks: *"STOP! STOP! What are you, fucking crazy!?? I'll talk!!"* All in good fun. Except, it occurred to me: what if instead of click, the gun went BANG and blew the guy's head off, first try? I used this gag in a film called *Kiss Kiss, Bang Bang* and it got a good response—because of the expectation in the audience's head. They were going: CLICK. The movie went: BANG.

Truthfully, there's a lot of awkwardness in violence. I hope we can sell not just our heroes' slickness and skill, but the haphazard nature of it. The seat-of-the-pants, "can't believe-THAT-fucking-worked" aspect. That too. At any rate, I'm hoping we can start to assemble on the same page. I urge you, don't be silent. Speak up. I'm more than willing to take credit for any good idea, especially yours. I'm also more than aware that it's not my 40-ft ass up on screen, it's yours; I will do my best to honor you.

My number is: --- --- ----. Don't be a stranger.

EVOLUTION NOT REVOLUTION

SHANE BLACK BRINGS *PREDATOR* BACK TO ITS ROOTS

"**Y**ou look in the mirror and you see you're not quite who you thought you were. You think you're 25, and then you're not. Part of me, just for sheer nostalgia, wanted to go back in time and reinvigorate that kind of movie I would have stood in line to see on a summer day at the National Theater in Westwood, Los Angeles. Go make the ultimate sort of summer movie that we liked when we were kids. That's it for me. It's time travel."

The Predator is also a homecoming for writer and director Shane Black, 30 years after the then new kid on the block was tapped to rewrite the script of the original *Predator*, but who ended up taking a supporting role in the movie instead.

"It was originally called *Hunter*," says Black. "It was just about a hunter from the stars, a lovely little script written by two surfers in Newport Beach, Jim and John Thomas. People like to meddle. They said, 'It's a good script, but can we jazz it up a little?' It really didn't need jazz-upping. 'No, please, come on. Come on in and just maybe put some jokes in or something.' But I still wasn't interested. So they said, 'We'll put you in the movie. You can actually fly with us down to Puerto Vallarta, you can be in the film yourself.'

"At that point, I said, 'What the hell. I'll come down. I'll be in the movie. Maybe I'll write a couple lines for you.' Then it came to writing the lines and they said, 'Would you like to do some writing?' and I said, 'Actually I'm just an actor here.' I completely blew it off. I was kind of a jerk actually, but all in good fun because I didn't think that they needed a rewrite."

"Shane was brought in to do some work on the script," remembers producer John Davis. "He had written *Lethal Weapon* and was an amazing writer. He really didn't want to do it, so it was subterfuge. We thought we would bring him in, give him a part, and once we got him in Mexico we would get him to do a little bit of work. But he said, 'No, you hired me as an actor in this movie and that's what I'm going to do.' When that became clear to all of us, he was the first one killed. He didn't last very long. So it's ironic that he's come back to write and direct this, because he has a tremendous and long history with *Predator*."

ABOVE: Shane Black (left), with Ira Napoliello, senior VP of Davis Entertainment (center), and Jonathan Rothbart, SFX supervisor (right) on the set of the film.

ABOVE: "The greatest thing was the dreads because the dreads really defined it... There wasn't anything about it that was corny, and I think that's the hardest thing to do when you create a creature from another planet."
Producer John Davis on the Predator's enduring appeal

PREDATOR LENS

58.47.22

ROLL: 100   SCENE: 429   TAKE: 1

DIRECTOR: SHANE BLACK

CAMERA: LARRY FONG ASC

"There was an emotional connection because of his attachment to the original material, and with that comes a vested guarantee that he will take it to the next level because he cares about it," agrees executive producer Bill Bannerman. "It has come full circle and he's now being given the responsibility, and he wants to take on that challenge to take this to another level, a level that's more intelligent. A lot of films tend to be dumbed down for audiences, which they shouldn't be, and Shane will never go in that direction."

The first thing Black did was draft in Fred Dekker, his old friend going back to their UCLA days who he'd been working with for three decades, to co-write the script. "Shane had been there since the get-go and felt an affection for it and wanted to do something that serviced the idea and the mythology in a way we hadn't seen since the first movie," says Dekker. "So, for instance, I knew Stan Winston, I did a movie with him. We stayed in touch on and off until he died, and he was a genius. The actual Predator is one of the great movie monsters of all time, without question. But it always bothered me that it was essentially humanoid. He was bilaterally symmetrical, he had two arms, two legs, he had a face. I wanted to make a plot point out of that. And so that became the story."

"We talked about updating *Predator*, being very respectful and tipping our hat to the lineage and history, but updating it," explains production designer Martin Whist. "We take the original as a base and bring a more contemporary feel. Predators, from 1987 to now, have grown over time. They've advanced, and so too has the audience and filmmaking. We wanted to bring the whole thing up to date and make it viable for a contemporary audience."

"Make no mistake, this is a sequel to the first two films," says Dekker. "We reference the first two films, the chronology and story that occurred in those movies. The way I describe it is expanding the mythology. Everything that's in those films still happened and still exists, but there's a bigger puzzle box that we're opening. One thing Shane and I talked about very early on is that the Predators have conquered interstellar flight, so they're not dumb. There has got to be more to their culture than just hunting. We became interested in the idea of different kinds of Predators. So we've pushed some envelopes in terms of the existing mythology."

Black also honoured the history of the Predator creature itself by bringing in designers and special-effects gurus Tom Woodruff Jr and Alec Gillis at Amalgamated Dynamics. This marks their involvement in a fourth *Predator* film, stretching back to the original in 1987, and they are key members of the team of collaborators Black has assembled to reignite the movie magic of that first film.

"There are lightning-in-the-bottle moments where everything just comes together," says Woodruff. "The dreadlocks, the scary helmet, and then you pull it up and reveal a scarier creature. The size of the creature, the fact it was not here to be reasoned with, just to kill people for sport. All of that stuff came together, it was a moment where all of it worked onscreen."

Capturing that lightning in a bottle once again is what it is all about for Black. "This one, I want people to get their tickets in advance. I want people who are fans to see that after 30 years of *Predator* films, we're taking it seriously again. We're devoting attention to making this an event picture. It's the right time to resurrect those 80s pictures. It's the right zeitgeist for me. Maybe the next picture I do is an intense divorce drama, but not this one. This one, I'm really going to have some fun with being a kid again."

BELOW: "To be able to spontaneously create on a set, both as a director and on behalf of the actors, I think that's where you get what Shane does so well. That's where you get movie magic." John Davis

BELOW: "The effects that work best are when it's a marriage between practical, physical, and visual effects." Jonathan Rothbart

THE FUGITIVE

THE PREDATOR SHIP

Space. Cold and silent. The Hubble Space Telescope gracefully arcs past, 350 miles above the earth, the platform from which man measures the vast field of stars. The moment of serenity is shattered as from a ripple in space-time emerges the Fugitive Predator's ship. The spacecraft, scarred and aflame from recent battle, shears through the telescope, showering burning debris into the atmosphere.

THIS PAGE: The Fugitive Predator (above) and concept art of its impressive spaceship (right).

"[THE SHIP] HAD TO HAVE A MECHANICAL UNDERSTANDING TO IT, BUT AT THE SAME TIME BE NON-LINEAR AND REALLY NOT HUMAN."

Martin Whist, Production Designer

"The ship is a very intricately designed spacecraft that doesn't reference anything that has been created in a manmade world," explains Bill Bannerman. "Our production designer, Martin Whist, had to reach into his creative archives and pull into the forefront something that Shane would like and that would embrace the mythology of the Predator world."

The ship had to be robust enough to endure long-distance interstellar travel, but at the same time be contoured for atmospheric entry and exit. Whist sums up the design challenges; "not too sharp, not too swoopy; organic everywhere. It had to have a mechanical understanding to it, but at the same time be non-linear and really not human."

According to director of photography Larry Fong, "Martin wanted to make sure it seemed like a foreign intelligence designed it." Whist confirms that brief. "I wanted to create a new language, a vernacular for the Predator based on his combination of being not from this planet, having the technology to get here, but being so grounded in

almost an analog way with the way he fights. This combination of being able to kick ass in a fundamentally bone-crunching way, while at the same time having this non-human advanced technology.

"I've never designed a spaceship," Whist goes on. "It did take me a while to get my head around the process. I went down a traditional route of illustrators and 3D design, and I just got nowhere—what I realized had to happen was, I had to basically own it myself in a three-dimensional way. I need to be in it, that's just my process. So, I essentially carved a scale model. I gave myself two weeks, and I just hid away in a sculpting room, and I carved a scale model of the ship and basically cracked the language, the design style in that method. After I carved it, we 3D-scanned it and it went into a computer to refine everything. Some of the elements were sent out to get CNC'd, but for the most part Aaron Jordan, my lead sculptor, and his amazing crew sculpted it by hand."

Computer Numerical Control is the process of using automated machine tools through pre-programmed computer commands. "It is

ABOVE: "The props had to be updated, sleeker. Not digital; it had to have a Predator intelligence, in a mechanical form, which applied to everything. To the ship, to the console in the ship, the design of the interior, the design of the exterior, everything Predator. We wanted to pull it away from tribal and make it this organic but intelligent tech-look."
Martin Whist

LEFT AND BELOW: "Martin Whist has done the Predator ships so spectacularly. These bio-mechanical sets, it's like being inside of a giant insect." Fred Dekker

a five- to seven-axis milling machine that can take a 3D digital model and mill that out," says Hamish Purdy, the set decorator. "It can be huge, it can be 12ft tall. And they can be programmed to mill a block of wood or a block of Styrofoam or a block of metal into any shape you want. It's similar to 3D printing. It's 3D carving."

For the interior of the ship, Whist looked to the new Assassin Predator it was designed to be operated by. "Color wise, I took my cue from the designs we made for the Assassin, which are these blacks and reds. So I used a graphite paint, which enables us to use very low lighting, but it still picks up form in the sculpting of the ship. You can keep the lights low, you can keep it spooky and dark and mysterious, but also see the thing. It's a set that's in keeping with the horror genre, making it a dangerous environment, while at the same time there's a ton of action that happens in there. It's a complicated set."

It's also a large set. "The Assassin is 10ft tall," Whist says. "So I designed the whole thing bigger than human scales. All the steps in the ship are Predator size, so it's actually quite awkward to walk on them; they are very deep. Everybody gets a real thigh workout."

BELOW AND LEFT: "My favorite part about the ship is the whole control section. There were huge controls right there with a giant chair. Any chair's big for me, but for these huge muscular men, they're small in it too. Being in the Predator's spaceship makes us feel like we're all tiny little ants." Jacob Tremblay

LEFT: "The front of the ship, the whole cockpit... had to be able to be lifted off of the front end of the set so they could bring a crane into the front." Construction coordinator Jesse Joslin

RIGHT: The interior design for the Predator Ship. A 3D model was hand-sculpted and scanned, with extensive secnic work done on set to replicate this.

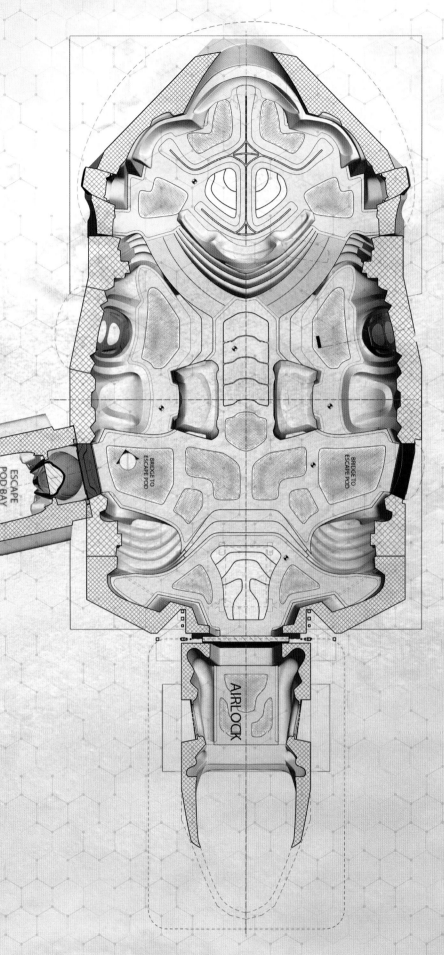

ESCAPE POD BAY

BRIDGE TO ESCAPE POD

BRIDGE TO ESCAPE POD

AIRLOCK

THE PREDATOR

At the helm of the ship sits one of the most iconic creatures in modern science fiction—a Predator in its biohelmet. "The idea of an alien hunter has shown enduring popularity," says Shane Black. "Maybe it's the costume, maybe it's the dreadlocks, but I think mostly the idea of something hunting you and you realize it's an alien from space and it's here because it's bored and it wants us to fight it so it can kill us."

For newcomer Brian Prince, who plays the Fugitive Predator in the film, the creature's relatability is key. "It's so close to human. The Predator is bipedal, hands with five fingers, two eyes; you recognize its silhouette as human, but it's more than human. He's huge, he has these mandibles. It's clearly alien, but it's not so removed from being human and I think there's something scarier about that."

"The design is so elegant and, like all the great monster designs, it immediately targets our subconscious," says co-writer Fred Dekker. "We look at this creature and we see some mirror image of ourselves but in a dark, scary, primal kind of way."

The cast have their own take. "It's kind of like a muscular Jamaican bipedal crab," says Keegan-Michael Key. "Like a caveman and a horseshoe crab had sex. In Jamaica."

RIGHT: "Seeing the Predator for the first time was pretty amazing. I've been lucky enough to work with some of the greatest make up, effects and creature design artists of all time, so I've been to this rodeo before. It's always a joy to see a beautifully made, real, practical monster." Fred Dekker

BELOW: Work on the Predator face mask at Amalgamated Dynamics in Chatsworth, San Fernando Valley.

OPPOSITE: "The dreads are very iconographic. One of the fun things in this movie was to ask ourselves, 'Why is it the way it is? What are the dreadlocks for?' And so we played around with that." Fred Dekker

Honoring Stan Winston's legendary design from the original feature, this Predator was a real practical monster. "Everything's becoming CGI now," says Dekker. "Yes, there's some CGI in our movie but to see them in the flesh, you can't beat it."

The Predator suits were created by Tom Woodruff and Alec Gillis at Amalgamated Dynamics, 30-year veterans in the monster-making business who have been involved in the *Predator* franchise since the first feature. "They've been masters of this world of creating textured monsters from prosthetics and the old-style rubber suits," explains Bill Bannerman, "but now they've taken it to a whole new level."

"This one we based on the original Predator, not exactly duplicating every detail and every spine and dreadlock, but enough that he represents the original type of Predator," says Gillis. "In designing a creature like the Predator, there's a lot of steps that you go through. It starts with a read of the script and a conversation with the director. And then we start doing sketches, where we bring together our team of six or eight artists, and we do anything from pencil sketches to Photoshop to ZBrush, 3D-sculpted models. That's when we move into the full-scale sculpture, which lets more design happen because clay is real. When the sculpture is finalized we make a negative mold of it, and from that we generate the foam rubber skin of the Predator. We generate the fiberglass cores of the skull and the skullcaps for the suit performers.

"And while that is all going on, we start building our animatronics. Strip away the skin and you have a mechanism that is made of fiberglass and metal, and has all the finely machined pulleys and pivot points. They have cables running from them to servomotors, which are all stored in the back of the character's head. The cables control the mandibles as well as the jaw.

"Eventually it comes together with both mechanical and art, and we start doing fittings on the actors. We're physically tailoring a suit, then painting the bodies happens, and the last thing is everything gets packed into shipping crates."

What's outside is every bit as vital as the inner workings of the suit, as costume designer Tish Monaghan explains. "The armor and the fabricated pieces are glued or Velcroed together so that in unison it looks like one piece. I did a count of the number of different pieces that were actually required and there are something like 11 pieces all joined together so it looks like a complete spacesuit."

The costumes required a lot of upkeep throughout the filming process. "Because of the kind of action that Brian has to do as the Predator, a lot of damage is incurred," says Monaghan. "After they finish filming for 12 or 14 hours, we would have a night shift going for the costume to be shipped back to, so that they could repair all the damage that happens so that it could be camera ready for the next day."

The opportunity to play a Predator was an unexpected one for Brian Prince. "I came into this doing parkour," he says. "Some people call it free running. It's the discipline of learning to move in, around, or through an environment by just using the obstacles around you and the human body. I had done a few stunt jobs in Atlanta, like a day here, five days there, but I had moved to Seattle and I was working at a gym doing parkour. One day I get a call and it was Lance Gilbert, and he's like, 'I'm the stunt coordinator for a movie and someone told me you were 6'10" and do parkour.' Super unexpected turn."

"Part of why the first *Predator* was so successful was because Kevin Peter Hall wore the suit and he was a 7'2", ballet-trained dancer," remembers Gillis. "That flowing movement that he would do and that gracefulness is what he brought to it. So 30 years later, when we heard that there was like a 6'10" guy out there who does parkour, we thought, 'Wow, this is fantastic.' And Brian's a phenomenal performer."

THIS PAGE: "The armor was created by Quantum Creation FX, which is Christian Beckman. He brought in a whole new vision creatively that gelled with Shane's vision to elevate the armor to another level." Bill Bannerman

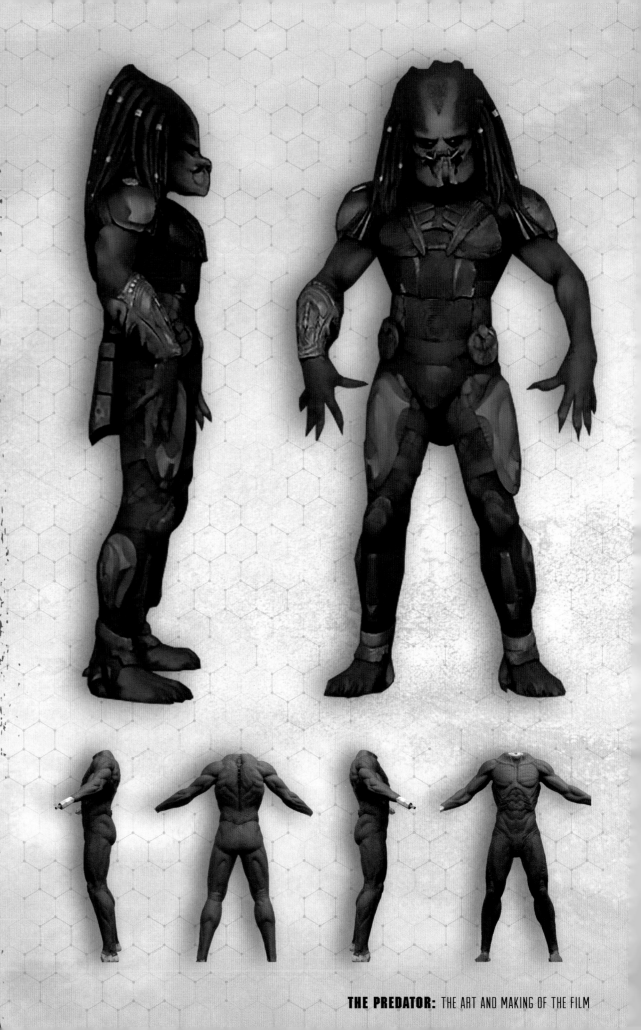

"THE ARMOR AND THE
FABRICATED PIECES ARE
GLUED OR VELCROED
TOGETHER SO THAT IN
UNISON IT LOOKS LIKE
ONE PIECE."

Tish Monaghan, Costume Designer

"WHEN WE HEARD THAT
THERE WAS LIKE A 6'10"
GUY OUT THERE WHO DOES
PARKOUR, WE THOUGHT,
'WOW, THIS IS FANTASTIC.'
AND BRIAN'S A PHENOMENAL
PERFORMER."

Alec Gillis, Amalgamated Dynamics,
on Predator performer Brian Prince

THE GAUNTLET

The Fugitive Predator's wrist gauntlet was one of the iconic images from the original films.

"With the new weaponry, we brought it to a more advanced state," says prop master David Dowling. "We're not saying that there's been a great lapse of time, but there's definitely been an evolution in the design of the weaponry, a little more purposeful, a little more refined. The gauntlets, instead of just being a top piece, we made it as a full wrap-around. We wanted to imply that it has many different powers that we haven't exploited yet.

BELOW: "The Predator wrist gauntlet lights up. There's different versions of it. One of them lights up. On one, there's no Kujhad. On another one, the Kujhad is connected. On this other one, you press a button and the Kujhad pops out. That one is my favorite." Jacob Tremblay

"The blades on the gauntlet are on a separate plate on top of the gauntlet that comes off. So we have two versions of it, one with the retracted blades and one with the extended blades. It's a visual effect to have them come out, and then when we need them out it was as simple as levering out the top plate and putting the extended blades in.

"They're all safe versions. Given their limited visibility it wasn't necessary to make actual metal ones. The finish that the folks at SAT [Studio Art Technology] did on them was exceptional. Most people have to touch them to find out that they're not actual metal. Very impressive."

"WE WANTED TO IMPLY THAT [THE GAUNTLET] HAS MANY DIFFERENT POWERS THAT WE HAVEN'T EXPLOITED YET."

David Dowling, Prop Master

ABOVE: "The original props had Earth tones, there's twang wrapped around them, they have this sort of pseudo-tech texture design to it. But I didn't want that. We didn't want tribal at all. We wanted a new mechanical look." Martin Whist

THE KUJHAD

"The Kujhad is what the movie is all about," says Martin Whist. "It's the primary device, it's what operates the ship. Sort of like the main brain. So it sort of tracks the whole movie."

Or, as Jacob Tremblay puts it, "The Kujhad is the key to the Predator's spaceship."

"It's the most important prop of the movie," Whist goes on. "I have an absolutely genius illustrator who started work on this a year ago. Fausto De Martini. I could just say 'Fausto' and everybody would know who he is. He's a freaking genius. We talked about the sentiment of it, the way I want the coloration, but he designed it.

"I tip my hat to him on that. We needed it to be as detailed and complicated and interesting as it could be. The design concept was to get away from the tribal with all of our props. We wanted it more technical, but gritty too. A rough industrial mechanical intelligence to it. It's gorgeous but it's not pretty. It's rough, you can knock it around and get it dirty but, at the same time, it has gorgeous lines and an industrial kind of detail.

"It was built by SAT in L.A., the best prop house in the planet, and it's the real deal. When you hold this thing it has weight, and it lights, it clips into the gauntlet, it's gorgeous. It's the real thing."

BELOW: "The Kujhad has a top plate that you push from the bottom, and inside are two batteries and there are two separate lights on it. We put some extra features in it just not knowing how we were going to want it to play. We toyed with the idea of making it remote-controlled so we could change the way the light behaves, but in this age of visual effects we just put some switches in it in a place that is quite subtle and it worked fine the old-fashioned way."
David Dowling

THIS PAGE: Views of the shoulder cannon, an iconic piece of Predator weaponry.

THIS PAGE: Views of the shoulder cannon, an iconic piece of Predator weaponry.

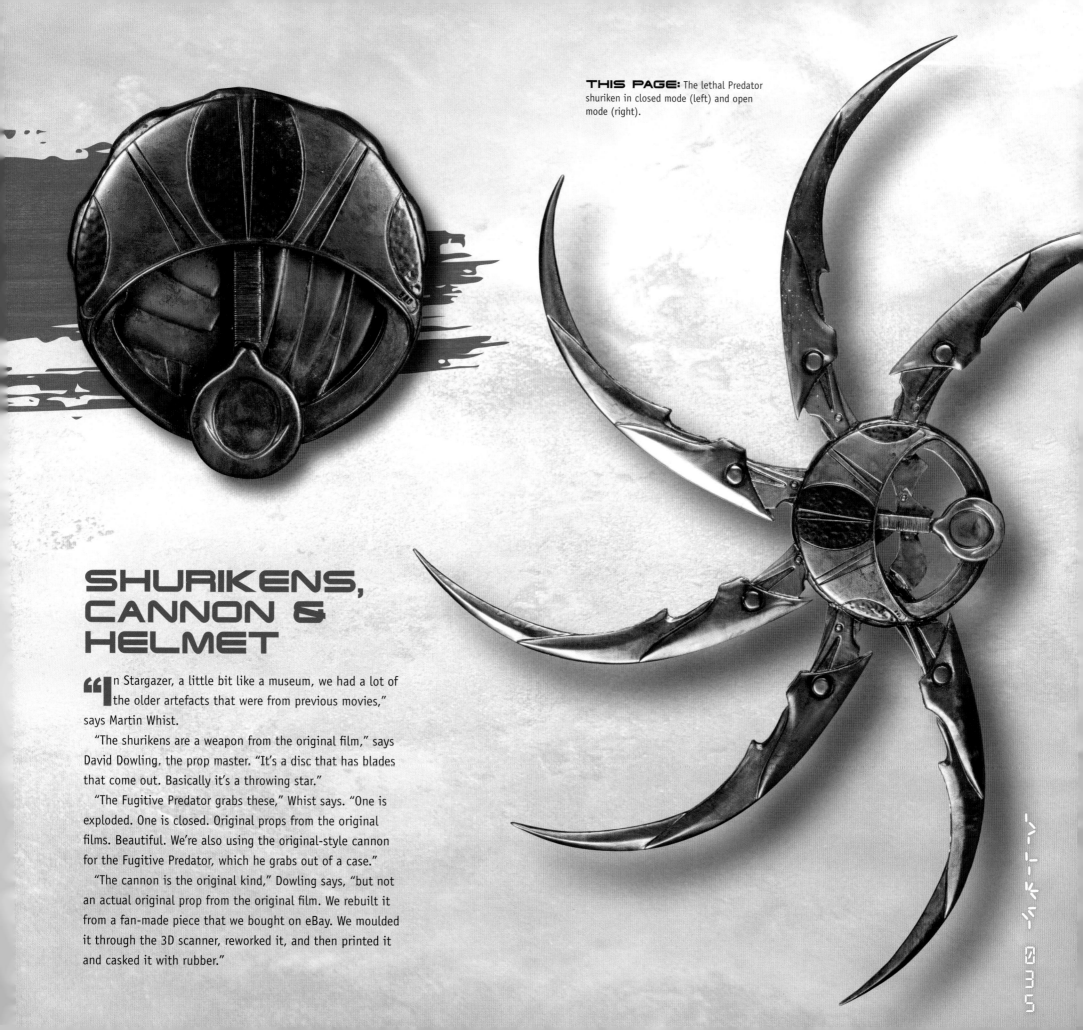

SHURIKENS, CANNON & HELMET

"In Stargazer, a little bit like a museum, we had a lot of the older artefacts that were from previous movies," says Martin Whist.

"The shurikens are a weapon from the original film," says David Dowling, the prop master. "It's a disc that has blades that come out. Basically it's a throwing star."

"The Fugitive Predator grabs these," Whist says. "One is exploded. One is closed. Original props from the original films. Beautiful. We're also using the original-style cannon for the Fugitive Predator, which he grabs out of a case."

"The cannon is the original kind," Dowling says, "but not an actual original prop from the original film. We rebuilt it from a fan-made piece that we bought on eBay. We moulded it through the 3D scanner, reworked it, and then printed it and casked it with rubber."

"THE MASK ITSELF IS A SIMILAR SHAPE TO THE ORIGINAL. WE WANTED TO GET AWAY FROM THE BLOCKISHNESS OF THE FRONT AND GIVE IT A LITTLE MORE DETAIL."

David Dowling, Prop Master

McKENNA

Estranged from his wife and son, Army Captain Quinn McKenna might be a lousy husband and father, but he's a good soldier. A security counter sniper in the Army Rangers, he supervises close precision engagements across the world and is a recipient of the Distinguished Service Medal and the Silver Star.

"McKenna is not really comfortable in his own skin," says Fred Dekker. "He's happier behind a sniper scope than he is having to deal with his son and his wife." For actor Boyd Holbrook, this is the crux of the role he plays. "You could break it down and say this is a story about a father and a son," he explains. "A father who's detached from the world, doing mercenary work in Mexico. A lot of McKenna's unhappiness comes from being estranged from his son. That hurts him a lot. You know, it breaks his heart. Nobody wants to hear, especially coming from your son, that you haven't been doing a good job. It's like they don't know each other. But we get to understand why they don't know each other, and we get to see how they come back together."

"He has this Steve McQueen kind of gravitas," Shane Black says of his leading man. "For a guy who's young, he has an old-school movie star quality. He's a true actor, a thespian. You see him walking around with headphones, he's listening to Dennis Farina talk so he can sound like he's from Chicago."

"I was fortunate to meet a stunt guy, an ex-sniper out of SEALs," says Holbrook on preparing for the role. "In my work as an actor, I like to play things that are foreign to me, sort of a novice anthropologist, getting to know different veins and tracks of life. So he got me on the beach 5am, Santa Monica down in L.A., and in the water, running, training."

BELOW: "Boyd looks too young to have gone through what he's gone through and be a soldier of this experience, so I aged him around the eyes, built in all the lines on his face, which during shooting he began developing naturally suddenly," jokes make-up designer Victoria Down.

RIGHT: McKenna confronts Stargazer private security at the Fugitive Predator ship crash site.

CASEY

An evolutionary biologist, Dr Casey Brackett is brought into the fold by Stargazer to help them figure out why the Fugitive Predator they're studying has traces of human DNA. What should be the defining moment of her career descends into mayhem as the Fugitive Predator escapes and Casey realizes Stargazer isn't what it first appears to be.

Initially, Olivia Munn turned down the role. "Usually in these movies, she has to be the love interest. It's all these men and they're fighting the alien, and she only exists if he exists. And I said no thank you." However, Shane Black persisted, laying out Casey's role as a key character, and after meeting with him Munn changed her mind. "Casey has her own storyline and helps figure out what's going on. She's actually needed for her brains, not because she's just simply a woman. That was important to me because of the micro aggression that is perpetuated in film pertaining specifically to women and minorities."

"Women characters have gotten a raw deal from the beginning of movies," says Fred Dekker. "I was really interested in doing a Howard Hawks woman, a woman who's every bit as good as the guys, who can give as good as she gets and is smart and funny." Shane Black agrees. "There are hints that she may be slightly unhinged or maybe even a bit alcoholic but, you know, all that's great because she's a tough-edged girl. She's not daunted by much."

Munn took inspiration from close to home when portraying Casey. "I based her on a few people but namely my cousin Angie, who is one of the smartest people you'll ever know. She does non-profit work around the world and she's in Afghanistan, and Somalia, and Rwanda, and we never know where she is, but we always know that she's in a place of danger where she is most needed. She's there helping people and [is] very passionate about what she does."

As Casey teams up with McKenna and the Loonies and faces off against the Predator threat, Munn found she had to develop a few new skills. "My character gets to go from living in a nice clean world with her dogs and being an intellectual and a scholar, to just being broken and beaten down and exhausted and diving on top of a Predator. I said the gorier the better. The dirtier the better. The scarier the better."

LEFT AND ABOVE LEFT: "At the beginning when you see Casey, she's wearing a beautiful coat and a nice shirt and scarf suitable to the environment that she was in. But, once she goes into the lab, she loses that and she ends up grabbing her own military jacket, her backpack, and her little flask of whiskey. She's definitely one of the team." Tish Monaghan

RORY

McKenna's son Rory lives with his mother, Emily, in the suburbs, a world away from his father's life as a Ranger. He is also something of a savant on the autism spectrum, possessing an incredible facility with languages.

"He goes to school, he likes chess, and he's really smart, but he gets bullied," says actor Jacob Tremblay. "He likes to figure out puzzles. He's good at figuring out the keypads on the Predator's spaceship and learning their languages."

When a package containing Predator technology is inadvertently redirected from his father's PO Box to the family home, Rory is drawn into the situation McKenna is trying to deal with and finally gets to see his father again. However, the boy's knack with the alien tech and language makes him a target for both the Predators and Stargazer.

"The kid has information and he is able to speak the language without speaking the language," explains co-star Sterling K Brown. "He has a mathematical mind that's able to comprehend things that have been beyond the comprehension of Stargazer: how to locate the Predator ship, how to open the Predator ship."

Or as Tremblay succinctly puts it, "The Predators are coming for me to get the brain."

Despite only having a handful of previous feature film credits, Tremblay impressed everyone on set. "Probably the most dependable actor on the cast, a one-take wonder," Shane Black says. Olivia Munn was similarly dazzled. "Jacob did a lot of work to understand and to be able to live in the skin of someone with autism. He did a really beautiful job with being understated, being subtle, and not making it into a stereotype in any way, just really gave it a lot of love."

Tremblay and Black had the opportunity to meet children with autism in preparation for the film. "Me and Shane had a chance to go to the Canucks Autism Center, and we made friends and got to hang out with some kids," remembers Tremblay. "Going to spend time with children with autism helped me learn about Rory would act and how he would move, and it helped me learn about stimming [stimulatory behavior exhibited by some people with autism, such as hand flapping]. And after we went, me and Shane discussed it and we really made a character."

RIGHT: "Rory hasn't really seen his dad in a long time, and his dad sends him this package, and it's all these cool Predator gadgets. That's special for Rory, because it's from his dad. And when he gets sucked into this adventure, he gets to see his dad again... His dad always tells Rory to be a big boy and grow up and to go and do stuff, like be strong. But Rory isn't really the athletic type. He's more into making things and fixing puzzles and chess." Jacob Tremblay

TRAEGER

As played by Sterling K. Brown, Traeger is certainly an antagonist to McKenna and the Loonies, but not necessarily the bad guy. "I never quite see him that way," says Brown. "I like the idea of playing someone who's not bad, or twirling his mustache, but is pursuing his own agenda that happens to be at odds with everyone else's. I think during the Cold War things were very concrete—good versus bad. This movie dances in the gray a little bit more.

"Traeger knows that McKenna has had an encounter with the Fugitive Predator, and he needs to keep these sorts of things under wraps. But he's not a bad guy, it's nothing personal—McKenna just happened to be in the wrong place at the wrong time and become privy to information that he should not have. Traeger's on damage control."

Traeger runs a shadowy covert operation known as Stargazer, based in a secret facility in Georgia. "Stargazer probably started off as being hand-in-hand with the CIA," Brown explains. "The intelligence that Stargazer has on Predators and their incursions on the planet is superseded only by the government. In fact, Stargazer gives the government that information. They're a subcontractor feeding information to the state, who trust them to act in a responsible way."

Acquiring alien technology has become a personal obsession for Traeger, however. "What may have started off as something that was truly altruistic, and may have been beneficial for man at large, developed into, 'What can I do for myself?'" Brown says.

John Davis says, "There is that group of people that believe they know better, who are driven by power, who are driven by money, who are driven by their own justifications. They are not part of the greater good as much as they are part of their own good."

LEFT: Sterling K. Brown as Traeger, who shares some memorable scenes with Rory (Jacob Tremblay). "We had this once scene in particular where Rory had to curse Traeger out. He had to call him an 'asshole' and Shane made him rehearse it over and over and over again. Jacob told me, 'I don't really think that you're an a-hole. I just want you to know that.' And I said, 'Jacob, it's okay. For this scene, you can think I'm the biggest a-hole in the world.' He's like, 'Okay, I will. But I don't really think that you are.' I was like, 'I got you. But you can, right now.' And he's like, 'I got you. But I don't.' When it was over, you could feel like the energy in his body had been sapped out because he's been doing something so wrong. He's just cute, man," says Brown.

THE LOONIES

"**W**hen I grew up, war films didn't really celebrate war," says Shane Black. "You hated the idea of war, it was horrible, but the camaraderie was what you celebrated, the sort of effortless cooperation and that trust among the men. What we tried to do is get that group of six guys that reflects what we found so wonderful about the first *Predator* movie; The guys and the way that they just formed this unit who have each others' back."

All veterans of recent conflicts in the Middle East, the men are struggling to adapt to normal life. "They all met in rehab where they were all dealing with the fact that they're marginalized, disenfranchised ex-soldiers who don't have command anymore," explains Black. "They've been phased out, they have physical and mental problems, but they are also gifted with certain skills that don't go away."

When they first appear on screen, the Loonies are on the prisoner transport bus awaiting the same fate as McKenna. Although the exact reason for this is never explained in the film, the cast and crew worked out a backstory for themselves.

"I'm going to take credit for this," says Tish Monaghan. "I was trying to figure out their backstory. For me, I have to have a reason in order to dress them, even before I start dressing them. So what I decided was that they were all in a group therapy meeting and they come there regularly. They'd been complaining for months about the bad coffee."

"We keep on complaining for week after week, and it falls on deaf ears over and over again," says Keegan-Michael Key, running with the idea. "Guys, the coffee is terrible. Why is the coffee so terrible? Can we just have good coffee?" Thomas Jane adds, "Finally somebody wigs out, throws a coffee urn, punches somebody, throws a chair. We all get into it, and the next thing you know the MPs have grabbed us, thrown us in shackles and thrown us on a bus."

"They're all each other has," says Black. "The group already clings to each other because when they're alone their heads go to very strange and bad places. And so it's only through contact with people who keep them steady that they can build up steam again and go on one last mission. One which wasn't sanctioned or ordered by anyone, one in which they found themselves inexplicably thrown but one that they take to and say, 'You know what, no one really thinks much of us. In fact, everyone's counted us out. They think we're all nuts. So you know, as long as we're all off our meds, why don't we all go a little crazy and kill this thing?' It's kind of fun."

LEFT: "It's about the six guys who aren't government employees. They're the forgotten soldiers—misfits. They're all broken. They're all guys who for one reason or other were deemed untrustworthy and they got kicked out of the easiest job in the world to get, which is soldier in the US Army. But for whatever reason, they found each other. These oddballs with unbelievable combat skills, but some kind of attitude problem, sort of a Dirty Half Dozen, have come together in this one." Shane Black

WILLIAMS

The sergeant of a Special Forces group in the Air Force, Gaylord 'Nebraska' Williams is haunted by the things he saw and the things he did during the Enduring Freedom campaign. "In my mind, he was in charge of his unit and he made a bad call," says actor Trevante Rhodes. "He got everyone killed, and so he's lived with that."

"I'm a huge fan of the John Carpenter films," says Fred Dekker. "I love *Assault on Precinct 13*, I love *Escape from New York*. I think *The Thing* is his best picture. And I conceived Nebraska Williams as the John Carpenter character which he ripped off of Howard Hawks. So it's me ripping off John Carpenter ripping off Howard Hawks."

A suicide survivor, Williams carries his past with him wherever he goes courtesy of a gunshot scar on his head. The small details in make-up and costume, like Williams's tattoos and the lighter he is always seen playing with, were essential for Rhodes to build his character. "Each tattoo is memorabilia in the sense of the journey of his life," Rhodes says. "He has tattoos on each of his fingers that say sorry. Stenciled on by him, saying sorry to the unit that he got killed."

"He's keeping a record of his fallen comrades," explains David Dowling with regards to Williams's lighter. "We had a lighter engraved with the names of those characters, all of them. It's a pretty good character piece because it's just one of those little subtle things, it's not just any old lighter."

The first line Williams says in the movie is, "Got a smoke?" An homage to *Assault on Precinct 13*, Rhodes picked up on it and worked it into the fabric of his character. "If you listen carefully, you'll hear him coughing throughout the movie," Dekker says. "What Trevante did with that line is, Nebraska has lung cancer."

"He tried to kill himself quickly before," says Rhodes, "and so now he's smoking to kill himself in a slower manner."

"That was a wonderful actor just taking a line and turning it into a character," says Dekker.

RIGHT: "Williams's scar [from his suicide attempt] is in his hair line. It's cut out, so where the scar is his hair is actually cut down and there's no hair in there. Then the scar is placed and attached on top with makeup. It's a bit of a deal for continuity. He needed a haircut twice a week." Debra Wiebe

FAR RIGHT: "In feng shui, you need a big object in a room, otherwise it has no kind of balance. Trevante just being there, being quiet and watching and smoking his cigarette, that speaks volumes." Fred Dekker

"THOMAS JANE ALWAYS LOOKS LIKE HIS BLOOD PRESSURE'S TOO HIGH, AND HIS EYEBROWS ARE ALL OVER THE PLACE, AND HIS HAIR'S A MESS."

Victoria Down, Make-Up Designer

BAXLEY AND COYLE

"**W**hat's going on with this Ozzie and Harriet kind of couple?" asks Boyd Holbrook of the odd relationship between Baxley and Coyle. Older than the other Loonies, these two men are veterans of Desert Storm, the first Gulf War.

"Here's a guy who's just trying to live day by day, just happy he's alive," says Thomas Jane, who portrays Baxley as a shell-shocked soldier recovering from an emotional trauma. "After this terrible experience, Baxley, who's always been a little OCD in the first place—he's been able to control it, use it to make him a good soldier—develops conversion disorder and takes on Tourette's-like symptoms."

"Thomas Jane always looks like his blood pressure's too high and his eyebrows are all over the place and his hair's a mess," says make-up designer Victoria Down. "That's a choice, and it works with that whole Tourette's thing he has going on."

Known primarily for his comedic work, Keagan-Michael Key is in fact a classically trained actor, having earned his Bachelor degree in Theater at the University of Detroit Mercy, and his Masters at Penn State. However, as he explains, starring in an action picture isn't such a huge change in gears. "I am a very big fan of the *Predator* franchise. I'm one of those people who knows the entire canon. I know the *Alien vs. Predator* movies a little more intimately than most people.

"The thing that excited me the most was playing a character who is damaged," Key says of Coyle. "He has kind of resigned himself to a life that is mundane, that is quotidian, and that is completely diametrically opposed to the life that he lived in the military."

This is reflected in the details of his costume, as Tish Monaghan explains. "Keagan-Michael wanted to have Coyle's father's olive drag jacket on from the Vietnam War. This is a man that doesn't function very well anymore. We decided that he worked in a cold storage unit, and so he has a gray uniform shirt."

"There was a tragic event that took place in his life," Key says of Coyle. "He was a driver of a light armored vehicle, and in the midst of a firefight he got turned around and fired on another light armored vehicle that was in his brigade, and destroyed it."

"And he killed everybody except for one guy, and that one guy is me," says Jane. "So these guys hate each other, but they had to spend three years together in the courts, in the military courts signing affidavits, giving testimonies, saying this happened on this date and this hour, and getting the whole story down for everybody and all the MPs and the courts and paperwork."

"That's how they have a relationship," says Key, explaining the banter and fast dialogue between the two characters. "Baxley gets to a point where he goes, 'Well, I better figure something out because I'm gonna be next to this guy all the time, and what am I gonna do? Am I gonna kill him? He didn't mean to do it'. It wasn't that Coyle was drunk that morning and fired on other soldiers. It was that he panicked. And so that's what he's living with. That's what the jokes are—they're a salve or a tonic. But they're not a cure to the pain that lives inside of him."

FAR LEFT: Baxley and Coyle execute their ruse as part of their escape from the bus.

NETTLES

A helicopter pilot wounded in action, with his gang tattoos and crucifix Nettles displays a paradoxical combination of affiliations. "Nettles is Mexican," explains actor Augusto Aguilera, "and in Mexico religion is cultural. The majority of Mexicans that you meet are going to be Catholic. So it's just part of the way that Nettles was raised.

"Nettles has this helicopter accident," says Aguilera, delving into his character's backstory, "but this is well into his career, after being a pilot for a minute. He's done some great things, really courageous things, and he saved a lot of lives. But because of this accident, Nettles has a traumatic brain injury, and now he's not allowed to do the only thing that he really knows how to do. Shane gave me one note. He said, 'I think that you're kind of like Dopey from *Snow White and the Seven Dwarfs*.' And I took that and ran with it.

"I feel that it's important to touch on the fact that these people have been thrown away by the government and the military and in a lot of ways by society. Because these people return and communities don't really have a place for them so much. They have to start over. Right? Because these things don't transfer. Him being a helicopter pilot, now that he has this injury he can't be a pilot related to tourism or commercial flights or anything. So he's just kind of thrown away."

LEFT AND BELOW: Having started out in television, *The Predator* is Augusto's first major feature role.

LYNCH

An ordinance and demolitions expert, Lynch earned a medal for his time in Mosul. Unfortunately, his zeal for destruction saw a few too many things razed to the earth, hence his presence in the therapy group.

As played by Alfie Allen, Lynch is something of a card sharp. "They had a magician who taught Alfie card tricks," says David Dowling, "so we had to come up with a deck of cards that would be appropriate for that sort of unsavory character to use as a distraction. We went back and forth a few times and ended up manufacturing a set of interesting adult themed cards."

BELOW: "There were four sets of cards that were made. That anyone knows about anyway..." David Dowling

THE JUNGLE

Monterrey, north-eastern Mexico. Camouflaged and hidden in the undergrowth, McKenna runs the scope of his sniper rifle over a black SUV parked on a dirt road cutting through the jungle. The other members of his special-ops unit, DuPree and Haines, are in the vicinity keeping a close eye.

When a second SUV pulls up and two hooded hostages are brought out, three armed men climb out of the first vehicle. McKenna draws a bead on the one in a guayabera shirt. A drug lord. His target.

Finger on the trigger, about to take him out, McKenna is shaken by a deep rumble. Something comes out of the sky at pace, shearing off the top of a radio mast and heading straight at McKenna. Keeping his cool, McKenna re-sights the drug lord and fires. Before the body hits the ground, McKenna is leaping out the way of the new threat: a crashing UFO.

When production was confirmed for Vancouver, the filmmakers discussed different settings for the opening of the film depending on what locations they could find. "I had a concept for a jungle crash, a concept of an arid Mexico environment, a concept for the Pacific Northwest, and then the east coast, to the Maritimes or Newfoundland," explains Martin Whist.

Initially, the plan was to shoot the jungle scenes in the studio. "The opening pod crash was not a big sequence in earlier drafts of the script," remembers Whist. "It was peppered through as flashbacks, in smaller vignettes, so I felt I could pull it off re-dressing the swamp set." This involved converting the large set originally built for the film's climactic sequence. "It was the Okefenokee Swamp in Southern Georgia," says Whist. "And we were changing it to Mexico. So going from a swamp to a very lush green jungle."

BELOW AND RIGHT: McKenna in action during his ill-fated mission in the Monterrey jungle.

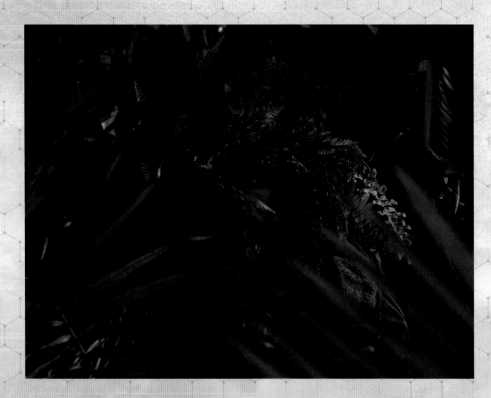

Ultimately, the decision was made to go big and shoot the sequence on location in the woodlands of British Columbia. "It's just going to look real and much better," explains executive producer John Starke. "Simply put, it's going to look very real. I'm from New York, and in these fabulous woods we have trees like I've not seen before. It's a beautiful woods, really looks eerie and perfect for us at night."

"The biggest challenge filming on location was that we were in the North West, Vancouver, which is a completely different climactic region to Mexico," says Whist. "So it did require finding a very specific spot. Luckily it's very wet there. It doesn't have the tropical foliage but it's wet so it's dense and green. I brought in all of the tell-tale banana leaves and palms and vines, and added them to the fern-covered Vancouver slopes. It worked out really well. We shot at night, which is going back to the original concept of the film, and that helped. It just makes it scarier and creepier. It's more interesting, denser visually. We rigged in the fire and explosions and

created the jungle scene at night very effectively. Turned out great."

The fire and explosions were the necessary practical effects for the Fugitive Predator's escape pod coming down to earth. "Filming the Mexico opening involved a very large forest burn in a remote location to simulate a UFO crash," says Alex Burdett, the mechanical special-effects supervisor. "We had had that forest burn going for over a week. Shooting on a stage and shooting on location, they both have their pluses and minuses, but something like the burn is easier to do outside than it is inside. You can go much larger with it."

McKenna finds the crashed escape pod empty, but retrieves the Fugitive Predator's mask and gauntlet from the site. Haines is found gutted and hanging from a tree, and a brief exchange of fire with the wounded Predator results in DuPree having a new hole blown through his chest. Discovering the cloaking ball in the gauntlet, McKenna turns invisible and escapes before Traeger and his goons arrive in a black Sikorsky to sanitize the scene.

ABOVE AND RIGHT: "McKenna's out on a job in Mexico when a Predator spaceship crashes and lands. He's not aware of the events of the original film. The government knows what happened, and that's been covered up. McKenna's a soldier doing his job, and he stumbles across this. He needs proof, no one's gonna believe him, so he needs to get this [helmet] back to the states." Boyd Holbrook

LEFT: Concept art of the Fugitive Predator's crashed escape pod.

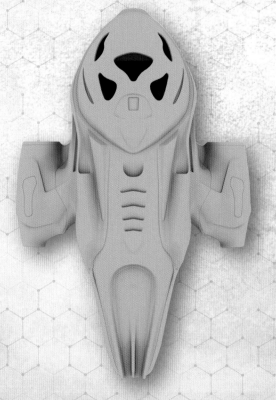

THIS PAGE: Computer models (far left) and final art of the Fugitive Predator escape pod.

MEXICAN TOWN

Bagging up the Fugitive Predator's mask and gauntlet, McKenna entrusts it (along with a fistful of dollars) to a bartender in a cantina, with instructions to give it to the US Embassy to send back to McKenna in America. Before Traeger's men can kick in the door, McKenna drops the cloaking sphere into a tequila and swallows it.

"We had many different concepts covered, and in the end we made the Mexican streets at the horse stables at the PNE [Pacific National Exhibition], at the Hastings Racecourse," says Martin Whist. "I built the interiors and exteriors of a Mexican cantina, and once all the extras came it was pretty flawless. So, very happy with that."

RIGHT: Concept art of the Mexican border town.

BELOW: McKenna walks into the small town with his precious cargo stored in his bag.

OPPOSITE: McKenna's psychological evaluation at the VA hospital.

PSYCH EVALUATION

Detained by Traeger and his band of mercenaries, McKenna is taken to a medical facility for what is ostensibly a psychiatric evaluation, but in practice an interrogation and a rubber stamping of an insanity diagnosis.

"The Reagan 80s was very gung-ho, pro-America, macho era, and it really works for the original movie," says Fred Dekker. "But we're living in a time now where servicemen are getting a raw deal and being sent to fight wars that they don't understand, and then when they come back they're treated poorly. We wanted to turn the macho commando idea on its ear and have our heroes be veterans who have been tossed aside. They have mental problems. McKenna's got a broken marriage, he's estranged from his son, and he's messed up a little. All of our Loonies are a little bit messed up. And we thought that was a much more interesting approach for the world we live in now as far as who are our heroes. They're the guys that are at the VA who can't get their meds because the taxpayers won't pay for them or the politicians are playing around behind their backs. And we thought those are the guys that we want to be our heroes."

PROJECT
STARGAZER

FACILITY EXTERIOR

Recruited by CIA agents working for Traeger, Casey is flown to Stargazer, a covert base located deep within a hydroelectric dam, where captured Predators can be studied. "The Predators have been coming to Earth and hunting us here for a while, but now people have noticed," explains Shane Black. "The government knows what's coming know, they're familiar with Predators. They've established a defense agency dedicated solely to protecting us from, and preparing us for, a Predator incursion."

"They're one of these government agencies that should have a three-letter acronym like CIA or FBI or NSA, but they're an unmentionable," says actor Jake Busey. "So I don't know if Stargazer would be considered good guys or not."

"Stargazer was initially a top-secret government lab, very high tech, in which the Predators that we might capture could be studied," says Fred Dekker. "And what happened in the backstory of the movie is that the government was concerned that they needed some kind of plausible deniability, so they put it in the hands of the CIA which could then manage it with that kind of cover."

A classified and highly sensitive location, the facility is heavily guarded by private security contractors. "Everybody does black-clad Mercs," says Tish Monaghan. "When I thought of Stargazer and the coloration that they were going to use there, I didn't want such a stark contrast. So we dressed a few gray-clad Mercs, but it just didn't fly. It was looking too ordinary. Then Shane said he was thinking back to 1960s or 1970s James Bond movies and he said, 'How about a jumpsuit?' 'Okay, let's try a jumpsuit then.' And I think they look uber cool."

Exteriors for the Stargazer facility were shot at two different locations, merged in post-production to look like one place, as Martin Whist explains. "We composited Lulu Island, a wastewater treatment plant, which has all these interesting outbuildings, and silos, and ramps, and put it onto the top of the Cleveland Dam at Capilano Lake. A big reservoir of water and a gorgeous, intensely dramatic ravine. So in the movie you'll see this facility, which is a digital composite of those two locations, and then I've built the set, which is supposed to be beneath that."

"WE COMPOSITED LULU ISLAND, A WASTEWATER TREATMENT PLANT, AND PUT IT ON THE TOP OF THE CLEVELAND DAM AT CAPILANO LAKE."

Martin Whist, Production Designer

SECURITY HUT

"Stargazer is hidden, it's not obvious that it's a government facility," says Martin Whist. "It's this really interesting place, this massive dam with these fantastic gorge rock cliff walls. The entrance to it is in this old out-station with an elevator that goes down into the facility, so it's camouflaged. I built a small structure, maybe a little service hut, and Stargazer would have covertly come in and redesigned it, made it into an elevator which runs probably 100-plus feet. You will see the tracking of lights as you move down, but it's all shot on a static set. Originally in a static set on location, and then on stage where we had a lighting effect to simulate going down. It had edge lighting to make the whole thing look like it's on tracks to give a sense it has come down all that distance."

RIGHT: Early concept illustration of the Stargazer security hut/elevator.

BELOW: Stargazer security hut interior.

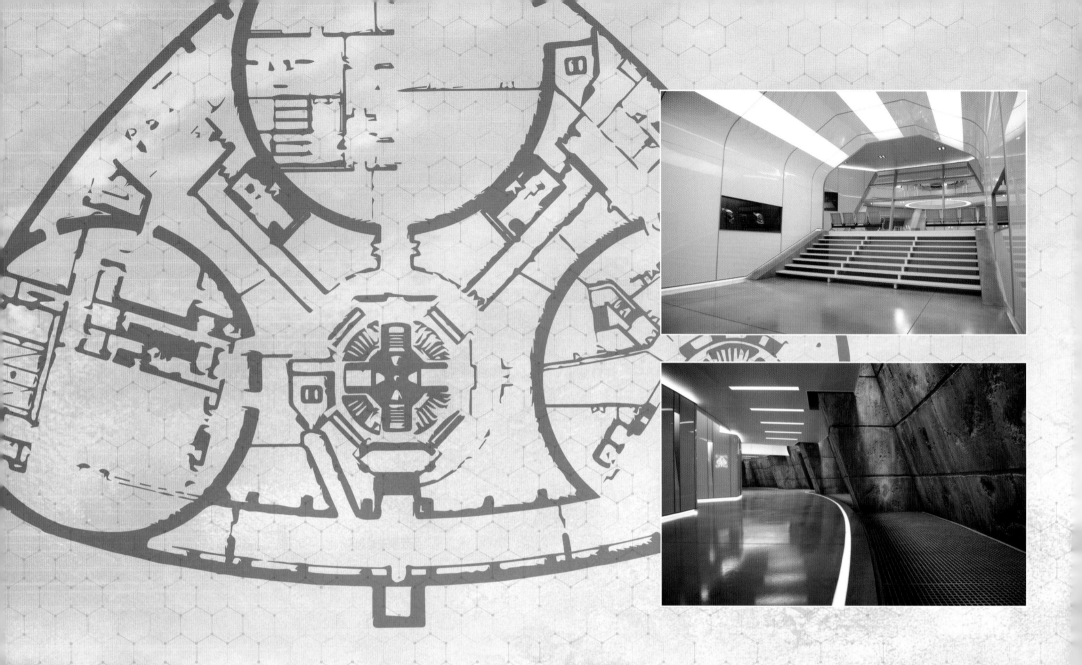

LABORATORY

The Stargazer facility is a labyrinthine subterranean complex beneath a water reclamation plant, bustling with technicians and scientists in lab coats and scrubs. "It's spectacular," says Fred Dekker. "It's a James Bond set, but with even more high tech."

The set was constructed on the vast soundstages of Mammoth Studios in Vancouver. "It is a wonderful facility," says Bill Bannerman. "It has expansive, free spaces where you're able to build very large, majestic sets without a huge compromise." Art director Michael Diner agrees. "That set itself is probably 20,000 square feet, 100 by 200 feet. Large space."

For Martin Whist, the process of designing a set on that scale began over a year before filming. "I had my illustrator, Jamie Rama,

do a preliminary sketch-up model and an illustration of the bones of this set in April 2016," he explains. "And the final construct was not very different in terms of the shape, with the circular aspect and the sunken middle. We have this long process of early concept development, and then there's a longer process of actual set design, which means drafting it in order to give it to construction. At one point we had probably 250 sculptors, carpenters, and painters going. It's a madhouse. The build for this set was scheduled for 18–20 weeks. Some stuff goes out, some new stuff gets started. We try not to start something and then have to undo it. I try to build in contingencies and get those decisions made and budgets approved before we start building."

"IT'S SPECTACULAR. IT'S A JAMES BOND SET, BUT WITH EVEN MORE HIGH TECH."

Fred Dekker, Screenplay Co-Writer

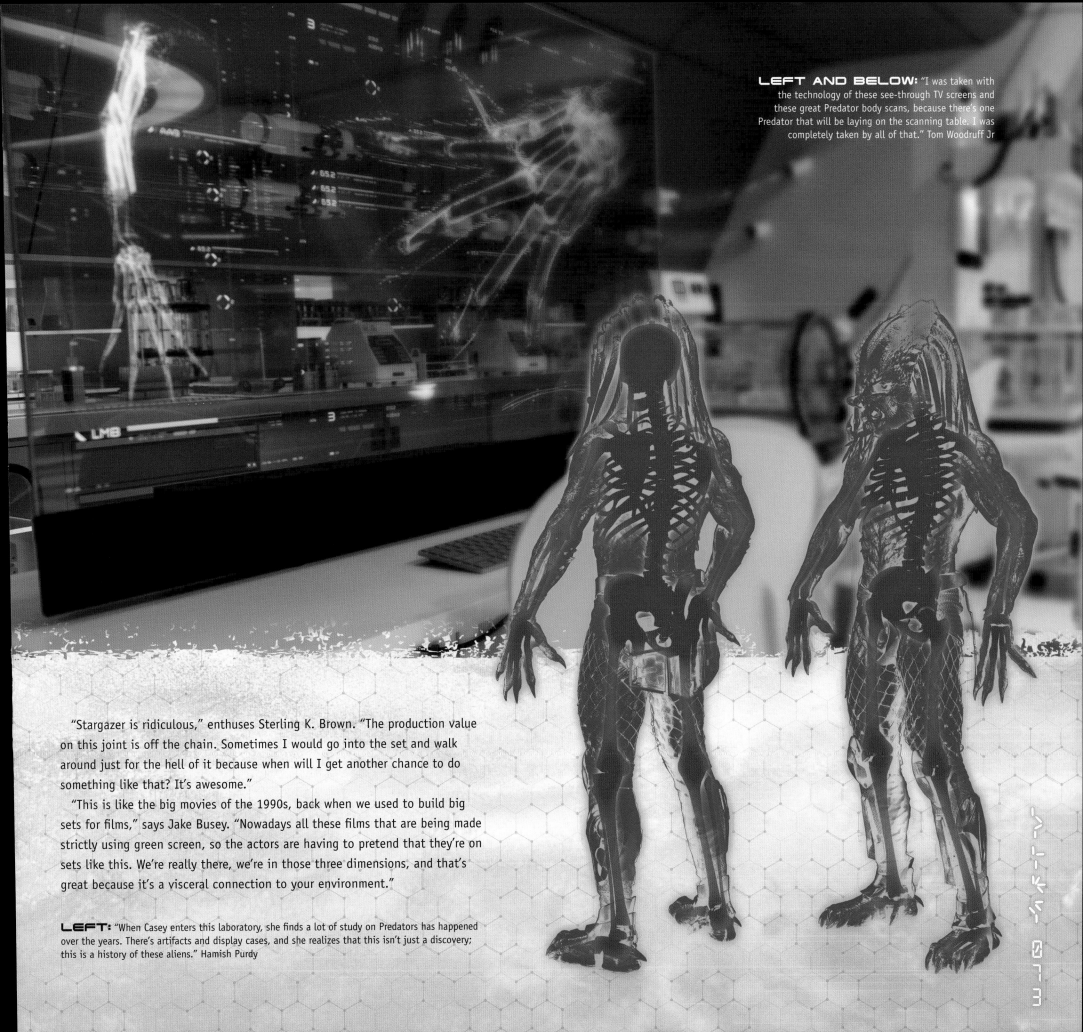

"Stargazer is ridiculous," enthuses Sterling K. Brown. "The production value on this joint is off the chain. Sometimes I would go into the set and walk around just for the hell of it because when will I get another chance to do something like that? It's awesome."

"This is like the big movies of the 1990s, back when we used to build big sets for films," says Jake Busey. "Nowadays all these films that are being made strictly using green screen, so the actors are having to pretend that they're on sets like this. We're really there, we're in those three dimensions, and that's great because it's a visceral connection to your environment."

LEFT: "When Casey enters this laboratory, she finds a lot of study on Predators has happened over the years. There's artifacts and display cases, and she realizes that this isn't just a discovery; this is a history of these aliens." Hamish Purdy

"One thing that Shane mentioned early on in the design was Ken Adam, Kubrick's designer," says Whist. "You can see from some of feel of this space that it is a nod to Ken Adam. One thing designers and moviemakers love tipping their hat to is the center ring in the *Doctor Strangelove* set, in the War Room."

The set was designed with lighting integrated into every layer to allow complete freedom for director of photography Larry Fong. "Nowadays with LED lighting it seems like there are endless possibility to what you can do," says construction coordinator Jesse Joslin. "There's over one kilometer of LED strip lighting in that set."

"I love that set," says Fong. "It was the most trouble to build, and it's very elaborate, but thanks to an amazing gaffer and amazing rigging gaffer the set almost lights itself. And that was the plan."

Before entering the laboratory-within-the-laboratory, where the real work is done, Casey must pass through a decontamination protocol. In an airlocked chamber she strips off and has the outer layer of her skin seared off before donning HAZMAT gear.

Although the Stargazer set was constructed practically on such a large scale, the production still seamlessly merged visual effects when required. "With the help of visual effects, a curved glass door will be animated, and glass from above will close and make it an enclosed chamber," explains Whist. "So the movement and the closing are visual effects and then, once it's done, construction and the art department will bring in the glass to have the static piece. That way, visual effects doesn't have to enclose the thing for every shot, because that becomes very expensive."

"There are some fun little things we do in the art department," says Whist. "They're not scripted, they're not asked for, but these embellishments that we add onto sets give it a little scope, give a little subtext."

"It's kind of outstanding," says actor Sterling K Brown. "If you look closely on the Stargazer set there is a directory that tells you where everything is inside of the complex, and you'll see there's a gift shop there too."

"What villainous underground lab beneath a dam couldn't do with a gift shop?" reasons Whist.

ABOVE: "We thought we were all done, and then Hamish [Purdy], Martin [Whist], and Scott [Calderwood—assistant decorator] came up with a wonderful new bed. They pulled it off in a short period, and we did very little to help them. It's this beautiful bed that can hold all of the Predator armor as we're taking it off. It looks fantastic. That's the kind of thing that happens all the time. 'There's not a lot of stuff left to do, we've got a week to kill now, may as well build something else'."
Jesse Joslin

RIGHT: Jake Busey as Dr Sean Keyes.

Dr Sean Keyes is a research scientist at Stargazer, driven to investigate the Predator threat by family tragedy. His father was a covert government agent in charge of the OWLF (Other World Lifeforms Taskforce), a precursor to Stargazer, and died in an encounter with a Predator in Los Angles 20 years earlier. In a case of life imitating art, Dr Keyes is played by Jake Busey, son of Gary Busey, who played Peter Keyes in the 1990 film *Predator 2*.

"It's not easy playing the son of my father," says Busey. "It's so close to home that it's hard to put a costume on and trying to make it a different character because it's me. So how do you do that? It's tough.

"As fathers and sons go, you'll notice that most sons don't emulate or mimic their fathers. You'll see a father that's maybe a boisterous guy, there's not much room in the house for the son to be boisterous as well. My father's character, Peter Keyes, was a very intense, very driven character. Sean Keyes is more of a devoted scientist who's after the facts, who's really searching for some answers, searching for what happened to his father and why. Why was his father killed? And there's retribution that's being sought in that."

THE PREDATOR BREAKS OUT

As Traeger receives word that another alien spacecraft is inbound, Casey's mind turns to the Predator strapped to the table. Crash-landed on Earth, alone and unarmed, where would you head for? The secret underground facility that has weapons from previous visiting Predators perhaps? Playing possum and allowing himself to be captured, the Fugitive Predator now makes his move, leaving a trail of bodies and mayhem in its wake as it breaks out of the laboratory.

"It demonstrates the speed and agility of this character that we really didn't get to see too much in the very first movie," says Hamish Purdy. "He was so camouflaged, we've never seen anything like it. Now we get to see what he can really do in these environments. So to that end, everything in the laboratory set is destroyed. We've got multiples of everything down there. Lots of glass to break away. All the equipment that I acquired for the movie, I had to own because of the huge fights that we had in there."

ABOVE: "There's a mask that's freaking cool, and then you take off the mask and it's even cooler. It's a creature that we recognize, that walks like us, that understands us, that has the same kinds of primitive impulses as a human being, but it's clearly not from here. And so the ability of a guy to look in the Predator's face and actually relate to it is what's interesting. The Predator has the capability of being an actual character." Shane Black

"NOW WE GET TO
SEE WHAT HE CAN
REALLY DO IN THESE
ENVIRONMENTS."

Hamish Purdy, Set Decorator

"I'M BEHIND THIS LAYER OF MASK TRYING TO GET AS CLOSE AS I CAN TO HITTING THESE GUYS WITHOUT ACTUALLY HITTING THEM."

Brian Prince (Fugitive Predator actor)

"The biggest challenge was dealing with the Fugitive Predator, dealing with Brian Prince with what he's wearing," says stunt coordinator Marny Eng. "It's difficult for anyone who's never worn a bodysuit and prosthetics with animatronics and contact lenses—there's so much that goes with it. You have to go to a parallel universe for the day, and not everyone has that in their toolkit. Not only is it physically and emotionally tough, it's a massive mental challenge.

"It's not nearly the same as putting on a normal costume, for so many reasons. The head weighs ten or twelve pounds, but it's back-heavy. The arms restrict movement, so he can only raise his arms so high. Then, the whole mental thing is huge. You're in that suit and you can't see, and you can't hear, and your skin's not breathing because it's covered with rubber. Coupled with that, a lot of times he's wearing a stunt harness underneath. And then you're working nights and it's pouring with rain and it's slippery, not only because of the rain, but because sweat is coming out from the bottom of the suit. It's exponential."

THIS PAGE: "The head probably weighs 9lbs. With the dreads and some slime we're up to 10lbs. You start putting fiberglass armor pieces on, which can stiffen the movement and add weight and reduce breathability. You have to be very mindful of the performer because you don't want to burn them out so that he's exhausted by the time he gets to the set." Alec Gillis

Eng and her team worked with Prince in the lead-up to shooting, preparing him for what lay ahead. "We didn't have access to the suit beforehand," she says. "We didn't know the exact size of the head, the weight of suit, or the footwear. The Fugitive Predator feet came out 16 inches long. So we had the poor guy in a 5mm wetsuit, we had bodyweights strapped to his torso, we had weights for his legs, we had ankle weights, we had flippers for his feet.

"We had a mock-up that props gave us of a helmet with an old Predator mask they got off a Halloween website. We were just trying to set him up, to give him as many tools as we could, because when anyone shines we all shine. It's all collaborative. We knew that was our biggest challenge early on—trying to set him up to win."

Predator weapons captured from previous encounters with the aliens are stored at Stargazer, giving the creature the chance to re-arm itself. "We are presenting the history of Predator weaponry, as though they have been gathering them for years," says Martin Whist. "They're all original props from the other movies, so we wanted to present those in display cases as though they're museum pieces."

The Fugitive Predator escapes the Stargazer site by stowing away in an armored personnel carrier. Prince recalls the complications of staging a fight sequence in such a confined environment whilst wearing the Predator costume. "It looks like the Predator's just fighting six guys, but really I'm fighting six guys with 65 pounds strapped to me, ten of it on my head. I'm squatting down so I can fit in the truck, and the mask is weighing me forward, and the lenses are completely fogged up, like a bathroom mirror after a hot shower. And my reach is extended out here with my fake talons, and I'm behind this layer of mask trying to get as close as I can to hitting these guys without actually hitting them, but it needs to be believable. It's a lot of mental gymnastics."

BELOW: "You see in the film, he smashes the display case and grabs the original helmet, and he's kind of like, 'Eh? Not so much.' So he takes the new one; it's updated, it's intense, but it obviously shares the overall form." Martin Whist

RIGHT: (clockwise from top left): Jake Busey as Dr Sean Keyes, meeting a similar fate to his father in *Predator 2*; Brian Prince harnessed up in costume on location at Lulu Island wastewater treatment plant; the Fugitive Predator dons his new helmet.

Hum Dinger MOTEL
CABLE T.V. & ICE COLD BEER

THE MOTEL

Casey, who had been pursuing the Fugitive Predator, accidentally shoots herself with a tranq-gun and is scooped up by McKenna as the Loonies flee the scene on stolen Indian Scouts. "We built a tow-rig for the principals to tow them through the shots," says Alex Burdett. "Then the motorcycle action was covered with stunt players."

The Loonies hunker down at the Iron Horse Motel and wait for Casey to awaken. "Casey waking up to see all the Loonies surrounding her was actually one of the first scenes that we rehearsed," remembers Olivia Munn. "It was originally written that she wakes up and immediately she's saying, 'Where's my phone? I don't trust you.' And the Loonies are saying, 'Stargazer want to kill you.' And she's like, 'Who are you? What do you know?' Like, very aggressive and not trusting them. She was definitely afraid but the way that the scene was, she woke up and just took charge.

"It was another moment where I was able to talk to Shane and say, she had just encountered an alien for the first time and she's chasing it. She tranquilized herself. She falls off a bus. She wakes up now groggy, banged up, in a seedy motel room full of strange men. I don't know how strong and confident she's going to be in that moment to just start ordering people around and telling them she doesn't care what they have to say. I asked Shane if I could take out all of my lines for a page and a half. And he was like, 'You want to take your lines away?' I said, 'Yeah, I don't think I need them.' Because, I feel like she would wake up and by this point the audience, they already know these guys are wacky and weird but not dangerous. They're the good guys."

At the motel, The Loonies acquire an RV and a cache of weapons from a redneck arms dealer. "Which conveniently explains why they're so well-armed," laughs Hamish Purdy.

"Yeah, with the magical RV we had the ability to say anything can come out of it," says David Dowling. "We were able to give them pretty much anything and pick weapons that matched their characters."

RIGHT: The Grouse Inn in North Vancouver was transformed into the Humdinger Motel for the shoot.

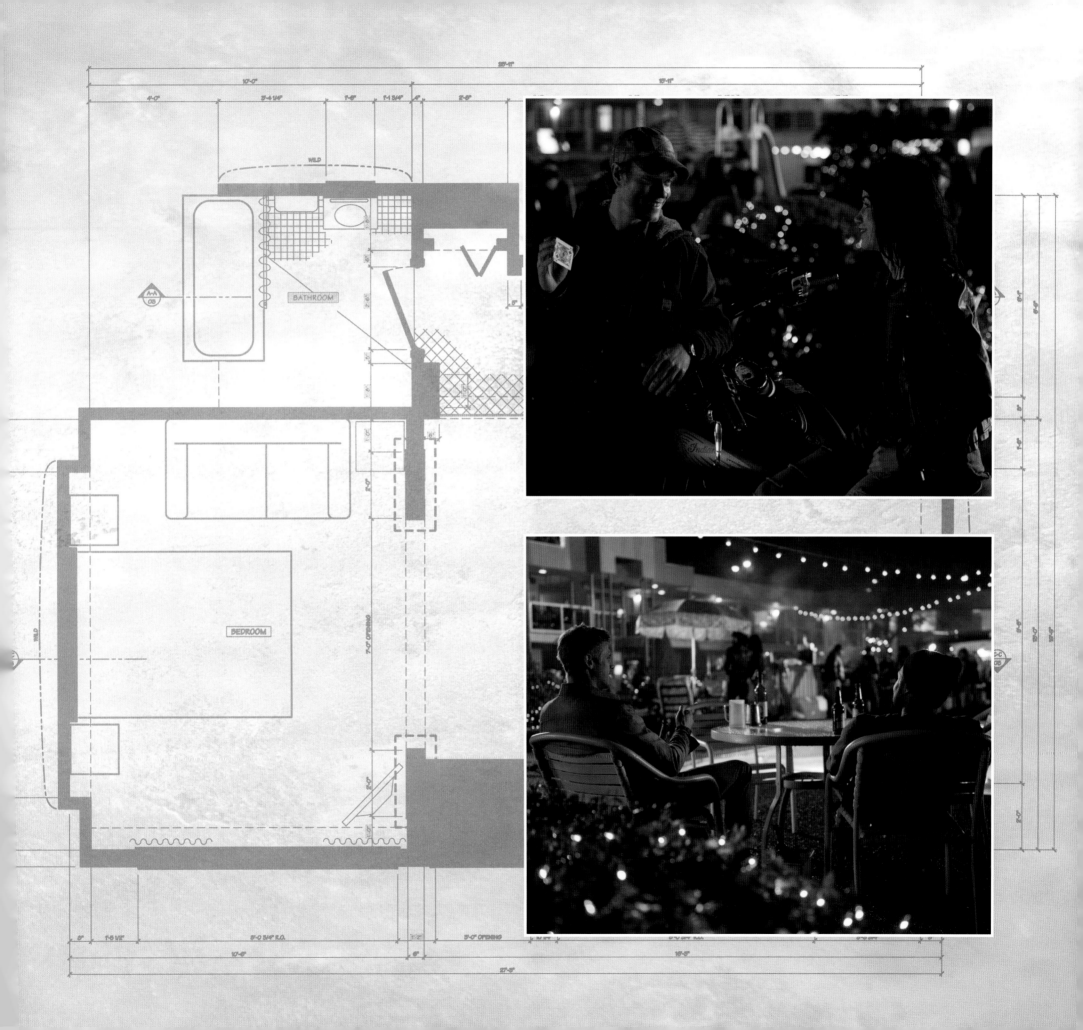

THE MCKENNA HOUSE

Realising the Fugitive Predator is searching for his missing gauntlet and Kujhad, McKenna leads Casey and the Loonies to the house where Rory lives with his mom, Emily. Effectively a single parent, Emily struggles sometimes with Rory, and finds an outlet in her painting. Well used to life as an army wife, surprise visits—firstly from Traeger and his mercenaries and then from her estranged husband and his motley crew—irritate more than worry her. Realising Rory is in danger, she knows McKenna is the right person to save him.

"The scene when the Loonies approach McKenna's old house, that was our first day of work," remembers Holbrook. "Shane just has a way of hinging a scene on what's really important. We rehearsed that scene and talked about it when there was no scripted dialogue. The actors all went to lunch and Shane went to his trailer, wrote, and after lunch handed us two or three pages. He'd located what was important, that we were there to find my son, but he also notched out all these little places, like Baxley's whole thing with his Tourette's or Coyle's comedic bits that bring it all back to what's at stake. Shane's a master of that."

BELOW: Baxley (Thomas Jane) can't help asking if Emily paints self-portraits.

FAR RIGHT: Australian actress Yvonne Strahovski as Rory's mom, Emily.

RORY'S BASEMENT

Rory's basement is not just his bedroom but his control area. "It's Rory's safe zone," says Jacob Tremblay. "It's where he can be himself."

Opening his father's package like it's a present, Rory fools around with the biohelmet and Kujhad. When the device comes to life, Rory goes to work on the displayed hieroglyphics, his prodigious aptitude for languages serving him well. Translating the alien language in his head, Rory gets a handle on the Kujhad and takes control of the incoming Assassin Predator spacecraft remotely, cloaking and de-cloaking it like it's a game, allowing intercepting F-22 Raptors to get a bead on it. Unfortunately for the air force pilots, they're still no match for Predator technology and get turned to dust.

Playing with the Kujhad and the gauntlet, Rory initiates a series of 3D projections. Graphics of a Predator ship's controls. Buttons, switches, gauges—a virtual-reality owner's manual whizzing by faster than the human brain can parse. Well, most human brains...

Unfortunately for Rory, his connection with alien technology is a two-way street. When the Fugitive Predator at Stargazer retrieves the biohelmet held there, he activates the helmet in Rory's basement and can see through it. See HIM through it.

"Rory is on the spectrum and so has an interest in numbers and counting," says Boyd Holbrook. "That makes it worse when he finds the Kujhad and the [Fugitive] Predator's gauntlet because he begins to actually figure it out and put the puzzle together. Through his own innocence and a child's pure curiosity he starts an avalanche of problems."

THIS PAGE: "Rory has all this cool stuff, like things that he can make, and these giant robot things, and he has a huge TV. He has chess tables in there. He has, like, four screens. Anything a boy like me would want." Jacob Tremblay

"WITH RORY'S
BASEMENT, IT'S
HIS CHARACTER. IT'S
ACTING, THE SPACE
IS ACTING."

Martin Whist, Production Designer

"One set you wouldn't think would be that exciting got me really excited," says Hamish Purdy. "Rory's basement, his inner sanctum, was a really exciting set. We had a lot of time to prep it, so we were able to put a lot of layers in there."

"We call them character sets," says Martin Whist. "It's almost more important than the Stargazer. A lab is a lab. Yeah, it looks nice but it's still a lab. With Rory's basement, it's his character. It's acting, the space is acting. It's one of those great environments where we were given the opportunity to create the personality of the character. And Hamish is absolutely brilliant at it."

"We had to understand why later on in our movie, Rory's able to fly our spaceship," explains Purdy. "How he's able to crack codes that no one else can crack. So to that end, I made sure that I had video games playing in the background, video games that required spatial intelligence. Lots of hand puzzles. I contacted a couple of companies that supplied brainteaser puzzles and they sent me lots of stuff. Crossword puzzles, Sudoku, anything that poses challenges like code breaking."

"To a decorator, they love these type of sets because it's the nuance and it's every little thing that tells the character of this young kid," says Whist. "At one point, we went a little too far. It looked fantastic, there was no problem, but it bummed Hamish when he actually saw Rory and how small he is. It was very subtle, but we had [him] too grown up. He's a savant, but the tools we had in there were for somebody who is a watchmaker, somebody who is older. It's a very fine detail. Rory takes apart computers, but he wouldn't have tools like that. He would have some scissors that maybe flatten into pliers at the end, and there would be one of his models next to it. So we dialed back his workspace. And that's what it is, finding the balance, the minutiae of who the character is. It was our opportunity to tell that story."

LEFT: Jacob Tremblay as Rory, investigating the alien technology his father sent back from Mexico.

TRICK
OR TREAT

Donning the Fugitive Predator's biohelmet and gauntlet, Rory sneaks out of the house and timidly roams the neighborhood. Surrounded by costumed trick-or-treaters and their parents, he watches other kids knocking on doors, nervous to try it himself.

"Shane has the courage to make it as odd and weird and unpredictable as possible in choosing locations," says Martin Whist. "Another director could have made Rory's neighborhood this nice quaint little American neighborhood, but he wanted it to be on the white trash side. There are boats and there's garbage and it's just a mess. For me, that was a victory. And it applied to every time we approached something, he didn't want it to be predictable, didn't want it to be what's been seen before. It goes to making it grounded and realistic. It's not that almost idyllic or utopian setting you would expect it would be, which can be a little movie-like. Shane goes the opposite direction. It makes it richer, it makes it more interesting, and ultimately more realistic."

ABOVE: The Trick or Treat sequence was shot on location in the Musqueam neighborhood of Vancouver.

RIGHT: Concept art of Rory's neighborhood on Halloween night.

> **"SHANE HAS THE COURAGE TO MAKE IT AS ODD AND WEIRD AND UNPREDICTABLE AS POSSIBLE IN CHOOSING LOCATIONS."**
>
> Martin Whist, Production Designer

Accosted by school bullies, Rory heads up the path of the least-inviting house on the block to escape them. A creepy place with no Halloween decorations or porch lighting of any kind, junk strewn across the patchy lawn, Rory finds the homeowner less than welcoming. Sensing a threat, the Predator's helmet jumps into life...

LEFT: Shooting the immediate aftermath of the house explosion on set (top) and with green screen (bottom).

ABOVE: A house with no treats gets tricked by Rory courtesy of the mini plasma caster in the Predator's helmet.

LEFT AND TOP: Wearing the Predator helmet and the gauntlet, Rory blends in amongst local kids trick or treating in their Halloween costumes.

OPPOSITE: Concept designs for the new Predator helmet, an integral mini plasma weapon replacing the shoulder-mounted plasma caster from the original films.

THE PREDATOR: THE ART AND MAKING OF THE FILM

"In the new helmet, the laser sight has actually transformed into a cannon," explains David Dowling. "We needed Rory to be able to fire at another character automatically and so we've modified the triangle sight to actually incorporate the cannon as well. So the helmet itself can detect a threat, sight it, and fire on it."

"We shot all of that sequence with the main unit," says Alex Burdett. "That was a large practical effect for the main unit. It was quite involved. That was a real house, and we built a façade on the front to protect it, and then blew the façade out. The homeowners were easygoing about it."

"The original Predator was this weird orange creature running through the jungle," says Martin Whist. "They had him in orange because it was going to be CGI and that was how they would track his movement. It was a weird shape, not scary, not anything like Stan Winston came up with."

"It was Jean-Claude Van Damme," recalls John Davis. "He was hired because the idea was the Predator moved in a graceful but aggressive way, and he was obviously a great martial artist. We were shooting for a day or two but it didn't work out, so then the idea emerged to get somebody big."

"In the Halloween scene with all the kids out trick or treating," Whist says, "We asked the costume designer, Tish, to have to have a kid dressed up in that orange original Predator costume. And she did it. If you look on the street, you'll see the original orange Predator. That's the best hidden little nugget, tipping our hat to the original Predator."

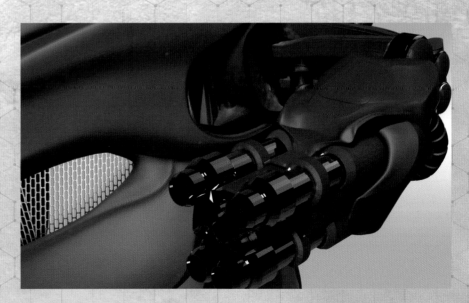

ENTER THE ASSASSIN

BASEBALL FIELD

After the Trick-or-Treat pyrotechnics, Rory escapes to somewhere he knows; the baseball field at his school. There he bumps into a kindred spirit and makes an unlikely friend—the pit bull that sometimes barks at him on his way home from school.

"The baseball field was shot on location and on stage," says Martin Whist. "It started on location, on the field outside the high school we filmed at, and we did the majority of it there. Then we rebuilt a portion of it on stage at Mammoth, surrounded by green, and shot the necessary elements."

"They planted a baseball diamond for like three days," remembers Augusto Aguilera. "With real grass, and some dude watering it and all that. I mean, it's like I'm gonna wake up one day and it was all a dream."

RIGHT: The baseball field set build on a stage at Mammoth Studios in Vancouver.

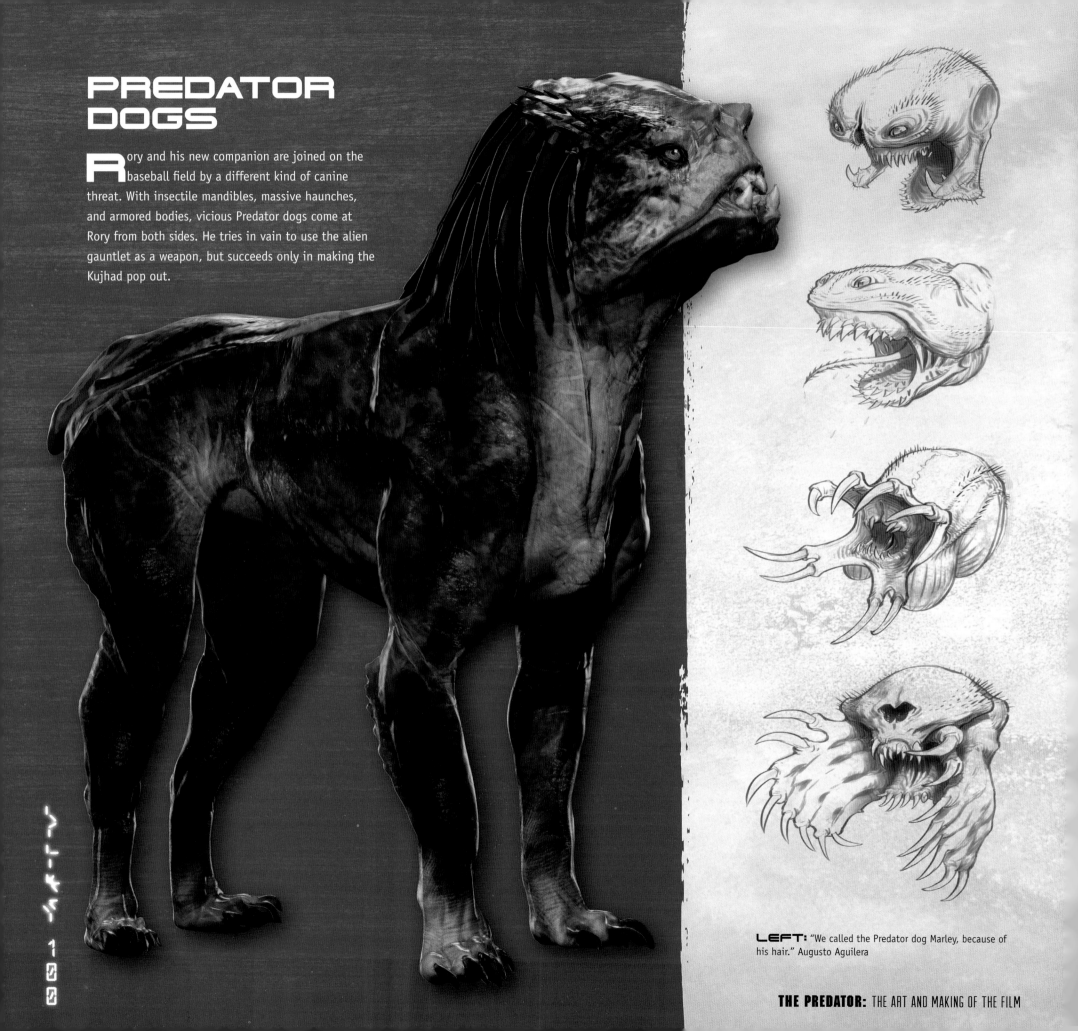

PREDATOR DOGS

Rory and his new companion are joined on the baseball field by a different kind of canine threat. With insectile mandibles, massive haunches, and armored bodies, vicious Predator dogs come at Rory from both sides. He tries in vain to use the alien gauntlet as a weapon, but succeeds only in making the Kujhad pop out.

LEFT: "We called the Predator dog Marley, because of his hair." Augusto Aguilera

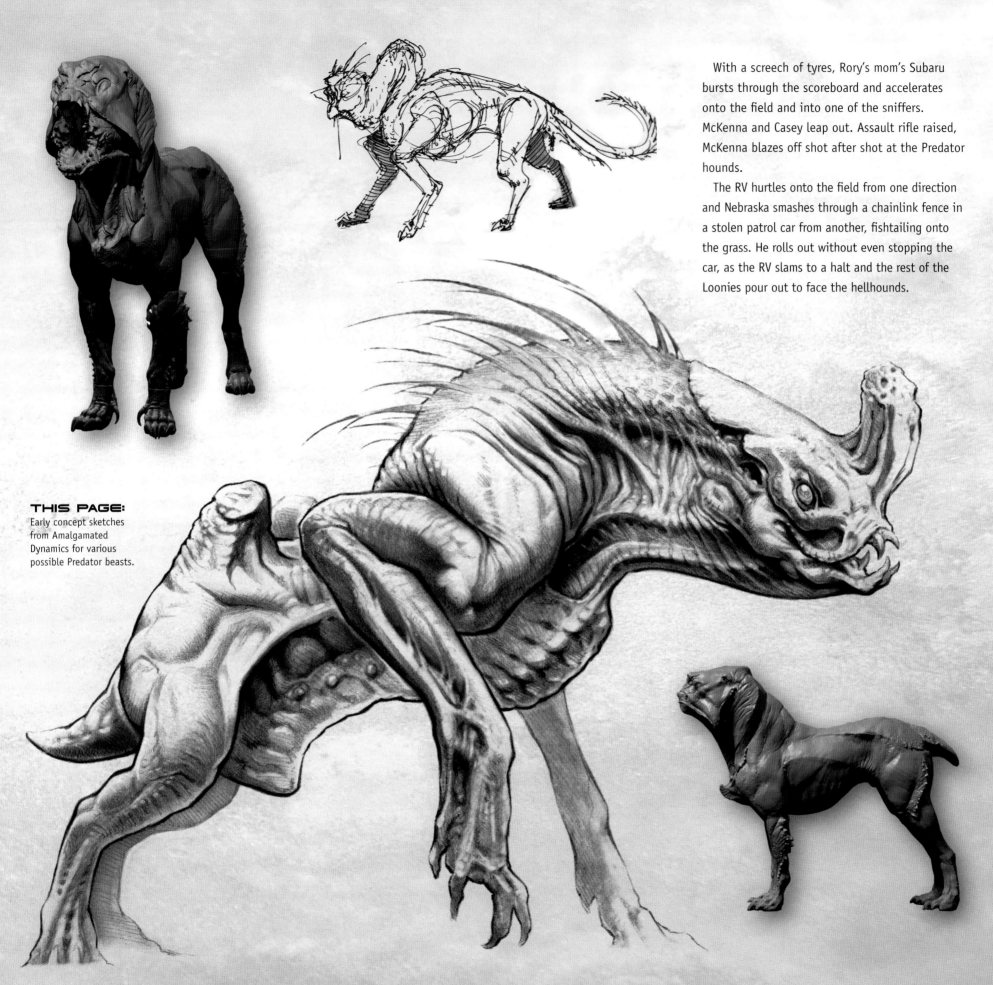

With a screech of tyres, Rory's mom's Subaru bursts through the scoreboard and accelerates onto the field and into one of the sniffers. McKenna and Casey leap out. Assault rifle raised, McKenna blazes off shot after shot at the Predator hounds.

The RV hurtles onto the field from one direction and Nebraska smashes through a chainlink fence in a stolen patrol car from another, fishtailing onto the grass. He rolls out without even stopping the car, as the RV slams to a halt and the rest of the Loonies pour out to face the hellhounds.

THIS PAGE:
Early concept sketches from Amalgamated Dynamics for various possible Predator beasts.

"The dogs are the Assassin's hounds," says visual-effects supervisor Jonathan Rothbart. "They go out, they find his prey, and if necessary they'll kill for him. And through the course of the movie we end up fighting them, and one of them gets lobotomized and attaches itself to Casey and kind of becomes her pet."

"These dogs are almost like your classic big dogs, and they have their own personality as well," says Matt Sloane, another special-effects supervisor. "And you get to see the [Assassin] Predator interacting with another creature almost fondly. It just gives them more depth, the Predator having his pets. It's another dimension. And the dogs are cute. They're big and horribly ugly, but they're cute in their own little Predator dog way."

"We got to design some of the digital creatures, and our favorite was the Predator hound," says Tom Woodruff Jr. "We worked with a great concept designer, Bryan Wynia, and there's this real otherworldly presence to this thing. It's a very weird-looking character, but it seems very real and really grounded. Definitely not of our world, but it looks like it exists within the physics of our world."

"This is something that I love to do in creature design. No matter how far out there the creature is, there are aspects that are reminiscent of our own world that I like to incorporate into a design, so that when a person is looking at it, they're not completely overtaken with something so foreign that they can't relate. So, to that end, this Predator hound has this armor that was somewhat like a rhinoceros. And this great underslung jaw that was somewhat like a bulldog. It's a bunch of physical elements that feel grounded in our reality, even though we're looking at them in a different way."

Amalgamated Dynamics Inc. created maquettes of their Predator dog designs that could be used on set, the creatures being animated in visual effects later. This can pose a challenge for actors during filming, but imaginative solutions were found.

"We had proxies so that we have eye lines and have that physicality between whatever creature is there in front of us," says Marny Eng. "If you've got ten people reacting to something buzzing around, and that something isn't actually there, the eye lines are all over the map."

BELOW: Sketches illustrating the evolution of the Predator dog's armor.

RIGHT: Stunt performer Trevor Addie using crutches for his performance as the Predator dog. The green dreadlocks aid the visual effects in post-production.

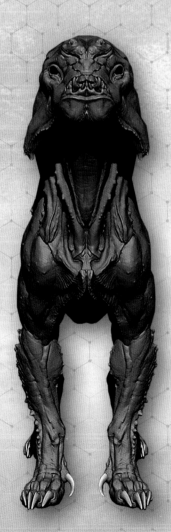

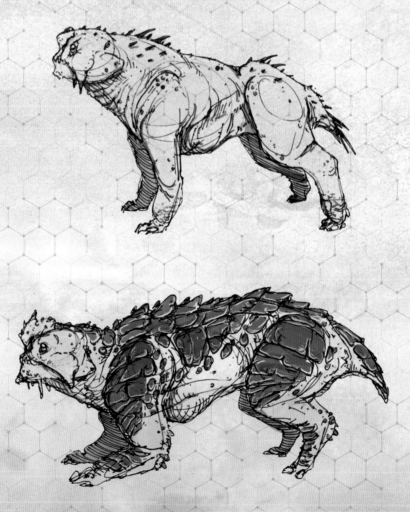

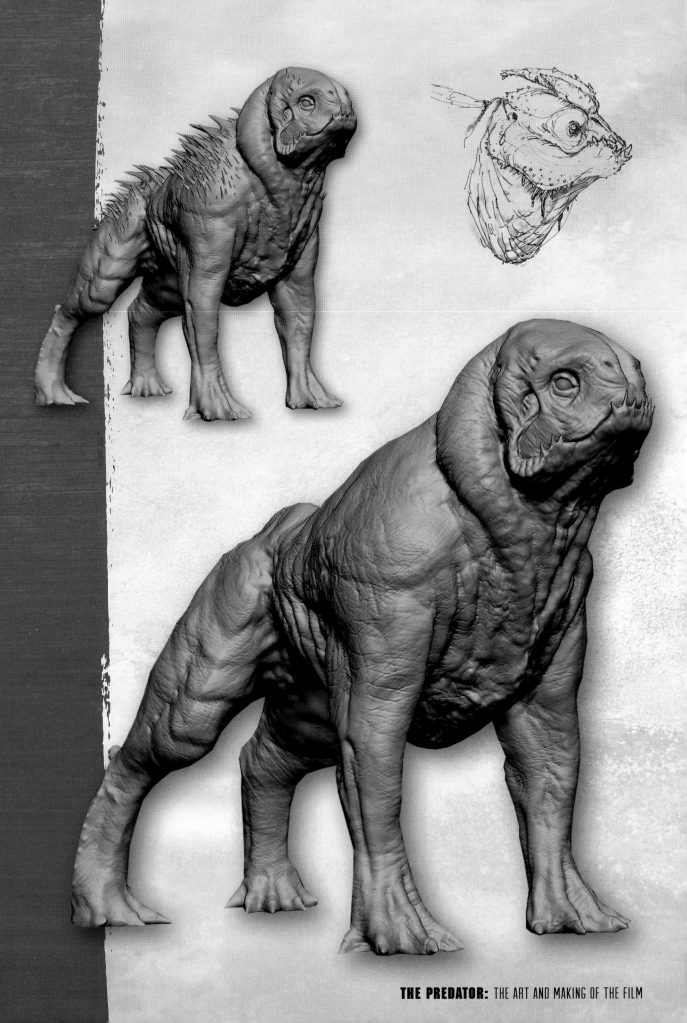

"We're standing there and we're looking at Trevor," says Augusto Aguilera. "And it's all in my mind. My dog is different from Thomas Jane's dog, which is different from Keegan-Michael Key's dog. We've all got different dogs, but it's just Trevor acting like a dog. Which is even weirder because you're petting him, and it's a person."

"As far as generally thankless jobs go, it's high up there on the list," laughs Trevor Addie, the stunt performer who stood in as a proxy for the dogs. "I'm in the movie, but I'm not. I'm going to be digitally removed. There's a lot of freedom in that, though. I can do whatever I want, and if they don't like it they don't even need to tell me to go again because they'll just erase it.

"Initially, they didn't know if they really needed to have someone there in the shot, or if they just needed to fill the space and decide what they were going to do later. One of the first scenes we filmed was one where they're playing fetch. Everyone was there. I didn't know what was going to be too much. I didn't want to distract anyone but the character—if you can call it a character— is just really a big puppy, and it's a serious movie. But I just committed. I decided I was going to be a puppy until they tell me not to.

"I completely dived in and after the first take there was a lot of laughter and I remember thinking, 'Okay, here's where they're going to tell me that was too much. Thank you very much, Trevor, but you just need to walk around on all fours.' But they didn't, and so I just kept at it. After a few set ups, crew members would come and tell me I was really brave. And I don't know what they meant by that. Was it was wearing the spandex bodysuit, or just fully committing to such a silly performance?"

RIGHT: Concept designs and sketches for the Predator dogs by Amalgamated Dynamics.

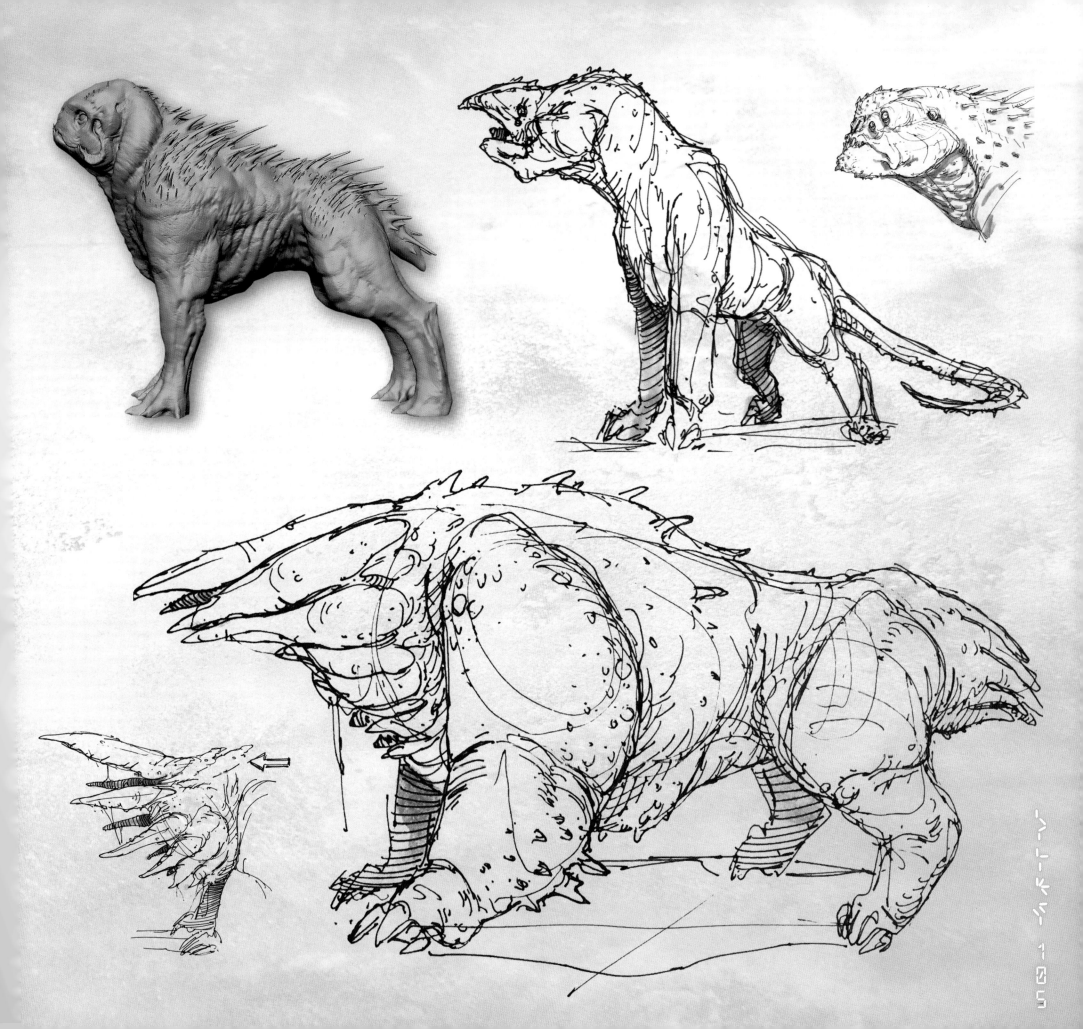

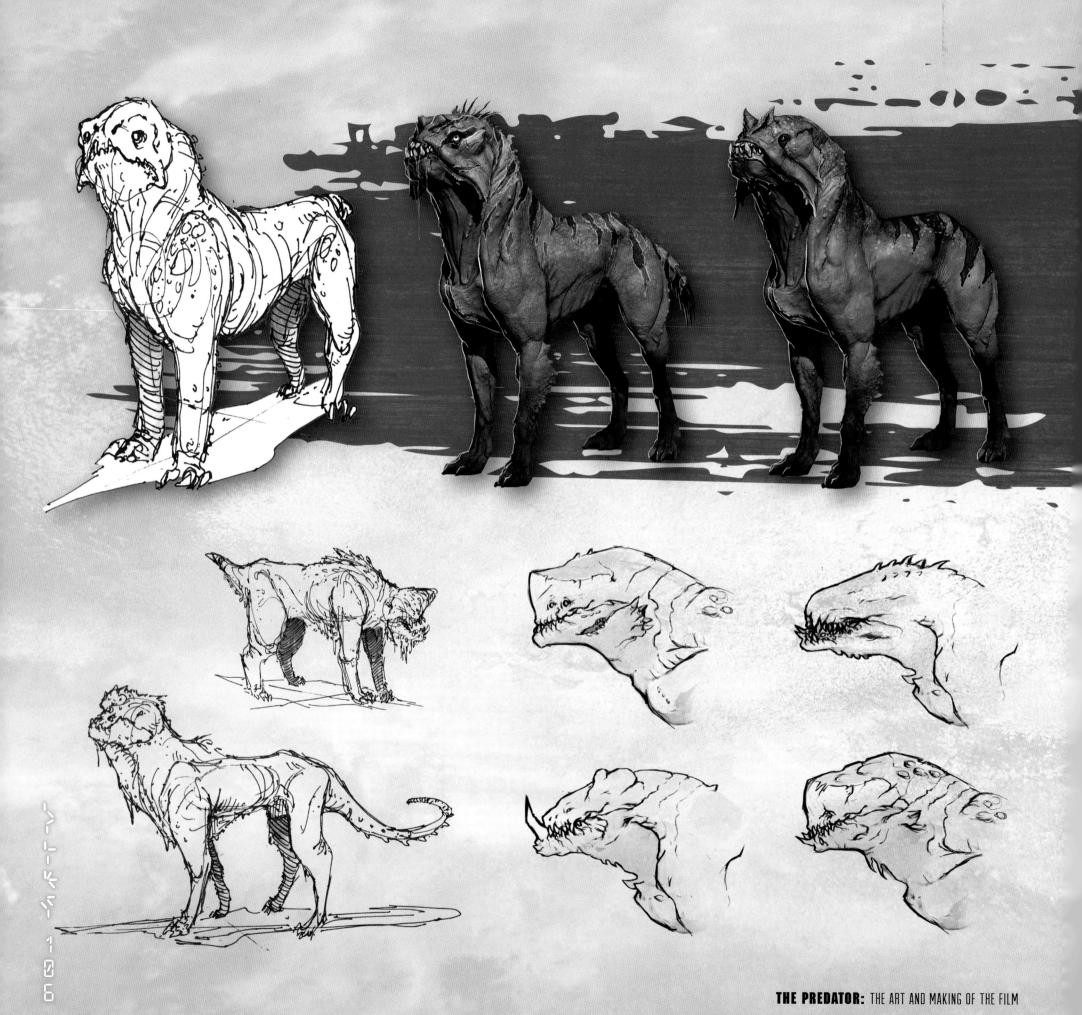

THE PREDATOR: THE ART AND MAKING OF THE FILM

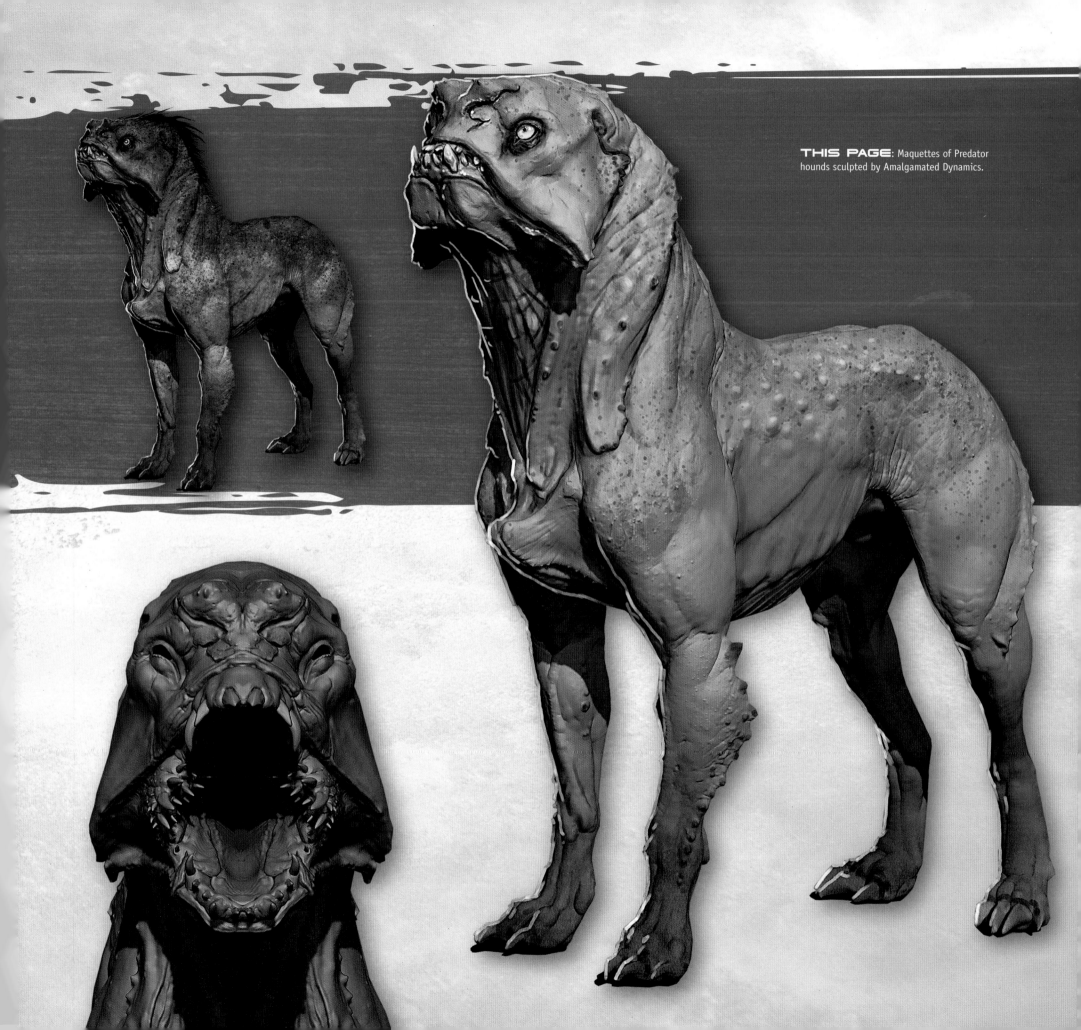

THIS PAGE: Maquettes of Predator hounds sculpted by Amalgamated Dynamics.

"THERE'S THIS REAL
OTHERWORLDLY
PRESENCE TO
THIS THING."

Tom Woodruff Jr., Amalgamated Dynamics

This new feather in his cap has Addie worried about being stunt-typecast though. "I doubled for mercenaries and a few other things as well. One day, coming in as one of the soldiers in the Stargazer lab, Shane Black looked at me and did a double take, and said, 'Oh, you're not the not dog today.'"

"Trevor's a great actor too," says Marny Eng. "Because not only was it a movement thing for the actors to watch, it was really like watching him act; watching his face, watching the way he did things. It was almost like that creature is another cast member really, so that people had that performance to play off."

Addie agrees. "You can see much more natural of a performance from the cast because they're responding to something that's there rather than someone telling them, 'Okay, now the dog moves and you tell

him to go back.' I think it just looks far more convincing. So as CG characters become more and more common, I think there are going to be good opportunities to play them like this. You get a great organic reaction from live actors and can completely delete the digital actor."

Olivia Munn's rescue dog, Chance, makes a cameo appearance in the film. "The scene where you first meet Casey, they have this park full of dogs, and they were trained but they weren't movie trained," explains Munn. "They were not wanting to stay or sit. They were barking. They were literally dragging me around. We only had so much time to do this, and Chance was actually in my trailer. And so my dog came in and plays the dog in the movie. And so I was very proud of him. The other dog couldn't learn his lines, so Chance came in and saved the day for everyone."

BELOW: Olivia Munn on set with her dog, Chance.

SHOWDOWN
AT THE SCHOOL

Regrouping after the battle with the Predator dogs, everyone makes for the RV. They pull up short when atop the vehicle appears the Fugitive Predator, firing a shot across their bow.

"We were shooting at a school when I first saw the Predator," says Augusto Aguilera. "I had no idea that we were going to see him. There were so many people surrounding this thing that we couldn't really see it, and then they parted. We all yelled. Or maybe only I yelled and that's the scream that I could hear. The thing was bigger than I thought it was going to be. It was more alive than I thought it was going to be. The mouth moved and the eyebrows moved. It was so surreal. I have no idea how to explain a moment like that. Somehow the whole thing had become real. I was actually making this film."

"It was our first big sequence," remembers Marny Eng. "We had a big gag of the [Fugitive] Predator getting thrown several stories, and there was other up-and-down wire stuff. So it was harnesses and the suit and really early in the day, even more challenging at night with the rain."

BELOW: Brian Prince as the Fugitive Predator.

In the film, the school is called the Lawrence A. Gordon Middle School, in honor of the former president of 20th Century Fox and producer of the original *Predator* pictures. The scenes were filmed at Templeton Secondary School, which is well regarded for its theater and film programs, and regularly appears in TV and feature productions.

LEFT: "At the school we used Robotics sparks. Where there was cannon fire we made the doors out of foam so that gave us the ability to have pyrotechnics that looked very big and very bright, but also we had our main cast in the frame so it was safe." Alex Burdett

TOP AND FAR RIGHT: Brian Prince in full Predator costume on set at the school.

Rory runs for cover in the school building, McKenna hot on his heels. The Fugitive Predator hunts them down in the corridors, overpowering McKenna as it seeks to reclaim the Kujhad.

"The stunts are amplified just because he's more than human," Marny Eng says of the fight sequences with the Fugitive Predator. "He's got some human DNA, but he's a creature, he's a beast. There was one instance when McKenna gets thrown by the Predator, and I asked Shane, 'Should he grab him and throw him, or should he just smack him?' And Shane said, 'Well, I think if he smacked him, he'd kill him, and we're not killing him here.' That solidified the idea of what kind of power this thing has. You have to stay true to those things and try to stay true to that storytelling so that it's consistent."

A new player enters the game. Looming head and shoulders above the monster we know and love, this Assassin is the next stage in the Predators' evolution. Rory and McKenna watch stunned as the two Predators go at it. It isn't a fair fight. Swift, relentless, and savage, the

Assassin Predator tears his smaller foe apart. The top of the food chain has just been raised.

The Assassin Predator returns to Rory's house, smashing through the floor into his basement room, leaving a trail of Stargazer mercenary corpses.

"Because the CG character is going to be so large, we needed a six-foot-by-six-foot hole for him to crash through," says Alex Durdett. "We built a large set on a stage. The exterior and upstairs were filmed at a real house, but the basement was a stage set."

"The basement was rebuilt as a match," remembers Martin Whist. "The scene with the Assassin was filmed later, so we had to build it again from scratch. We had all the set dressings stored, all the walls and everything. It's a pretty simple set as far as sets go, so we just rebuilt it, The only difference was, because the Assassin Predator comes through the ceiling from upstairs, we built a section of it rigged in such a way that that stunt could happen practically."

LEFT AND ABOVE: "When we build the Predator suit, whether it's a hero suit or a stunt suit, it's basically built the same. The only delineation between a hero and a stunt, generally, is that the stunt gets beat to hell during the movie. That's the one that needs to constantly be repaired. And then eventually it's gone, you can't save it, so you take one of the hero suits, and you make that a stunt suit." Alec Gillis

ASSASSIN PREDATOR

"The idea behind the Assassin is that the Predators are trying to develop and enhance the ultimate warrior in their race by genetic formatting and design," explains Jonathan Rothbart.

"They are not just hunting anymore," says John Davis. "They've been visiting this planet for years and years, and now their planet is starting to cool down and our planet is starting to heat up."

"Predator society has science and technology beyond ours," says Shane Black. "The species itself is obsessed with the concept of survival, which means genetics, eugenics, improving themselves through recombinant DNA splicing. So they don't hunt purely for the sport of it; the trophies they carry back have within them the DNA of every species they hunt from every planet they've hunted. The most deadly, adept, and capable version of that species. They'd find the best of every planet, they rip out its spine, and see if they can isolate traits and upgrade themselves into hunting machines."

THIS PAGE: The evolution of the design of the Assassin Predator.

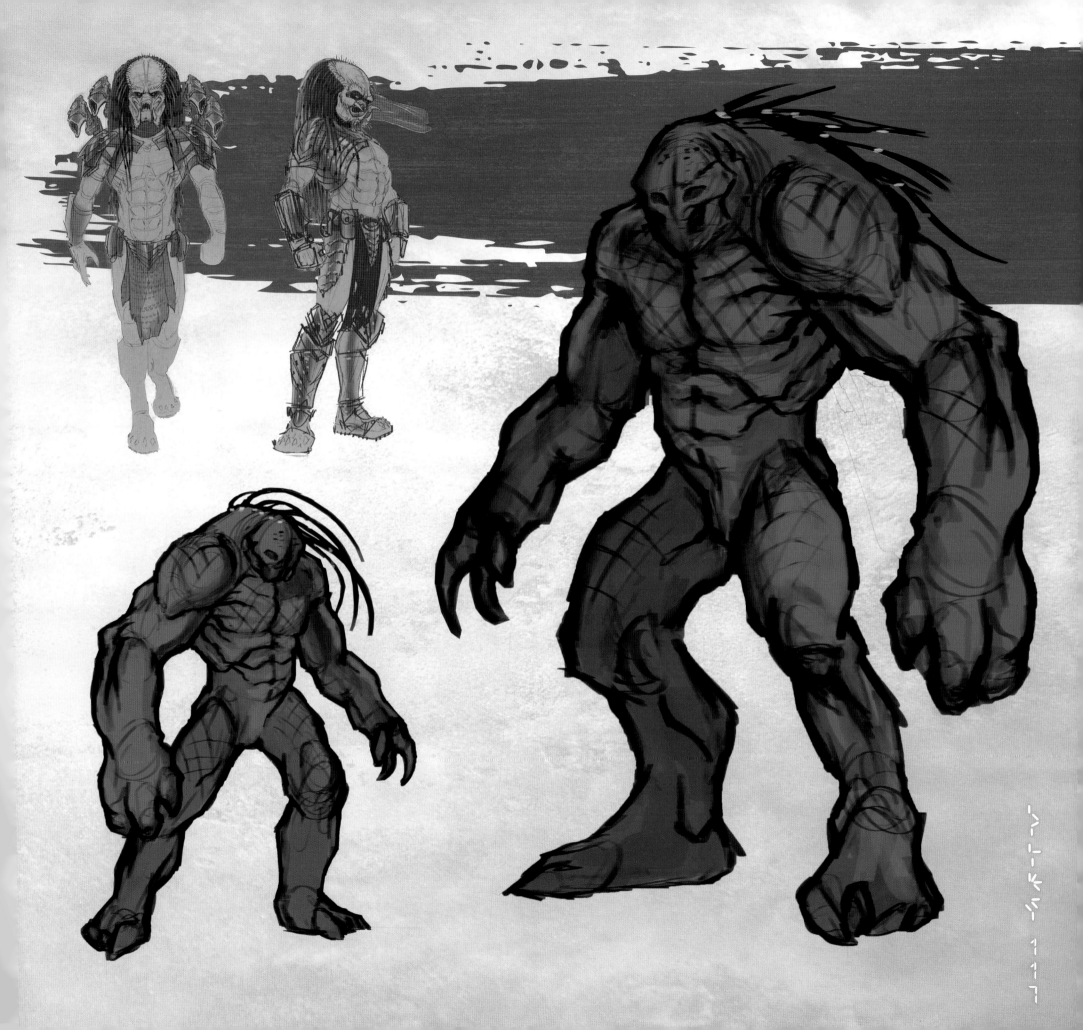

"HE'S A WEAPON
ALL BY HIMSELF."
Jonathan Rothbart, Visual-Effects Supervisor

"It's possible that they started these experiments early on," says Fred Dekker. "The Predator in the first movie may have had some element of human DNA himself and the original Predators might have looked very different, in the same way that we have Neanderthal and Cro-Magnon that resemble us but aren't us."

"The Assassin doesn't have armor," says Martin Whist. "He is armor. So he just has a very minor amount of clothing on him. His body becomes a hard exoskeleton of armor. Hand to hand he's just so vicious. He's the ultimate assassin and hunter. Rather than having weapons, there are attributes and weapons built into his own system."

"He's a weapon all by himself," confirms Rothbart.

This new Predator takes on two distinct looks depending on whether it's passive or engaged in battle.

"I work with a brilliant illustrator, an old friend of mine, Constantine Sekeris, who basically nailed it with our Assassin Predator," says Whist. "The passive color is akin to the natural earth tones of the original Predator, which contrasts with when he gets angry and goes into combat mode and turns black. At one point we were playing with tattoos, but it felt forced and didn't make sense. We didn't want to look tribal, which is such a human thing, but we wanted markings nonetheless. So not only does the skin texture turn into a hard shell—it's the armor—but his blood runs hot and turns ox-blood red. It's underneath the skin and it pulses through the skin, so he literally changes into a war machine, in full armor, with seething hot blood, and his eyes turn human and it just becomes this just awesome, menacing creature."

"He's big, and he's angry," says Matt Sloan. "We work out his personality through the film. He goes through a couple of stages as he and McKenna play this cat-and-mouse game. The Assassin gets more involved and starts getting a lot angrier, and you see the frustration. Basically, we try to assign personality to a CG character and give it a role, even though it's not physically there. Evolving that character so he'll come across as his own personality in the movie."

THIS PAGE: "The Assassin is not a huge departure. The fundamental make-up of the face, and the mandibles, and the dreads are all there. This Predator just happens to be advanced biologically as well; he's 10ft tall, he turns color and his body becomes armor when he gets in combat mode. He becomes this menacing, ferocious baddest of the badass. That's the departure." Martin Whist

"We wanted to do a meld of visual effects and practical in the best way, melding the two so that they seamlessly create the illusion of something very real," says Black. "Taking the Predator to the next level of deadliness, that required a degree of CG, but I don't like to overuse CG. I'm a fan of the old-school methodologies."

"Usually in pre-production we'll start pre-vising sections of the movie or important scenes that are going to be complex to shoot, just so that we understand and the crew understands how we're going to approach the actual filming," explains Sloan. "When you've got big creatures and big explosions, spaceships that aren't actually going to be physically there while you're shooting, you need to have it blocked out so everyone knows what will be happening in the end product. You have interactive lighting from electrics. The camera department need to know their framing. Every department is involved. The pre-vis is a great way of letting everyone see what the finished product will be before you've started filming so that we all have a target to shoot for."

"We had the visual-effects team there keep us in line if we didn't frame enough for a larger creature," recalls Larry Fong. "We had a guy with a strange rubber thing on stilts, sometimes on ladders, to get tall enough for the largest Predator. On some days where it's too complicated we had a mahl stick, which is a standard film industry thing. But the visual-effects people were always there to make sure we didn't make mistakes."

A model was constructed to represent the top half of the new Predator. Built on a mobile platform, just from the waist up it was as tall as a most of the cast members. "They made a model of the top half of the Assassin, all made out of latex or whatever," says Thomas Jane. "It's articulated with gears that they can move around and he can do stuff. And it's frigging huge. Its hands are as big as my chest. They didn't mess with it, you know? It's still the Predator. It's just a big giant mother badass Predator."

LEFT: The Assassin Predator in combat mode.

RIGHT: Full-sized model of the Assassin's head and torso used on set during filming. The actual creature was created with VFX in post-production.

TRAEGER INTERROGATES CASEY

At a rural farm, McKenna, Casey, Rory, and the Loonies go to ground to assess their next move. The peace doesn't last long, as Traeger and his mercenaries track them down. While some of the Loonies slip away, Casey, McKenna, Williams, and Rory are captured. Looking for the Kujhad, Traeger interrogates Casey.

"Olivia is wonderful," says Sterling K. Brown. "We had one scene in particular that was somewhat confrontational and it was written really well, but something didn't quite make sense to me. I told Shane, 'I'm gonna try something that's completely and totally inappropriate and probably won't work.' He's like, 'Those are my favorite choices.' I'm attempting to intimidate her in the scene and she won't give up the goods, and I do this thing where I sit on her. I just creep up and sit on her lap. Get really close and I let her know firmly that, 'You will comply.' Olivia was totally cool with how it went.

"You always have to make sure you respect your fellow actor and how you move forward together, that you're not forcing anything on your partner, you guys are doing it together. And then actually, when I tried to do something that seemed more standard, it didn't have the same sort of bright to it, so I'm curious to see exactly what makes the film. You give as many choices as possible and you never know exactly what is going to make the final cut."

BELOW: Shane Black directs Sterling K Brown and Olivia Munn for the interrogation scene.

RIGHT: Olivia Munn is harnessed up for a stunt in her escape sequence.

TAKING TO THE AIR

Realizing Rory is the key to locating and getting aboard the Fugitive Predator's ship, Traeger departs in his helicopter with the boy. Seeing this, McKenna makes his move and breaks free, Williams taking his cue and following suit. Casey proves she can take care of herself, getting a helping hand from the newly domiciled Predator dog too. The Loonies return with transportation they've liberated—a stolen news helicopter.

Filming the escape meant some stunt work and fight sequences for the cast. "At a certain level when you're doing wire work, you might take a couple of blows—I think I got kicked in the ribs a couple of times in the barn," says Boyd Holbrook. "Just by accident, of course," he adds.

"We can do the helicopter shots from an SUV," explains camera technician Lev Yevstratov. "We can extend the boom pretty fast and have the camera ten meters above the ground. We have a crane braced on the camera car, and on the end of the crane is a stabilization system with gyroscopes and accelerometers. This allows you to move the camera from any point to any point with speeds up to 100 miles per hour, or more. The car is made in Germany, the crane is made in Russia, and the customization is done in California."

RIGHT: Exterior shots for the interrogation scene were shot on location at a farm in Aldergrove B.C., east of Vancouver.

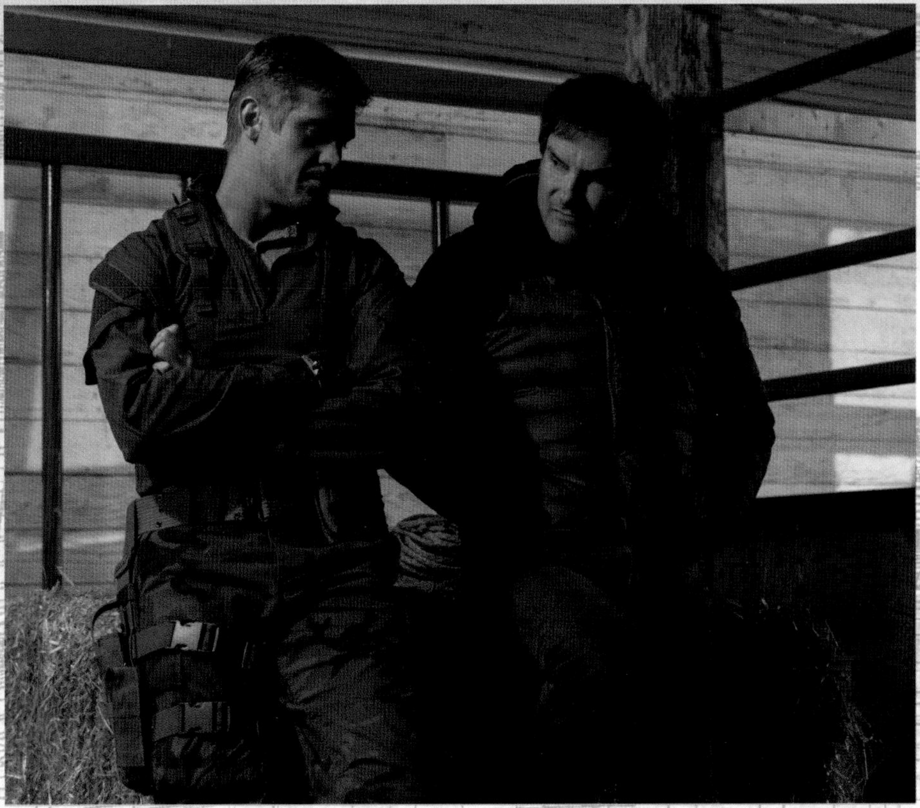

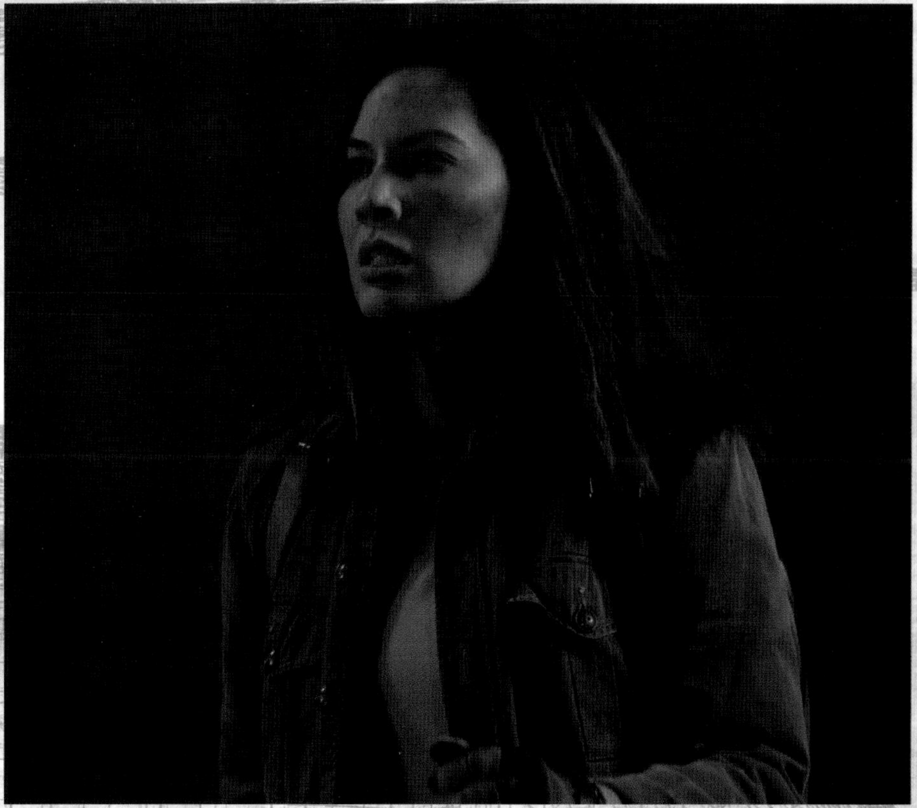

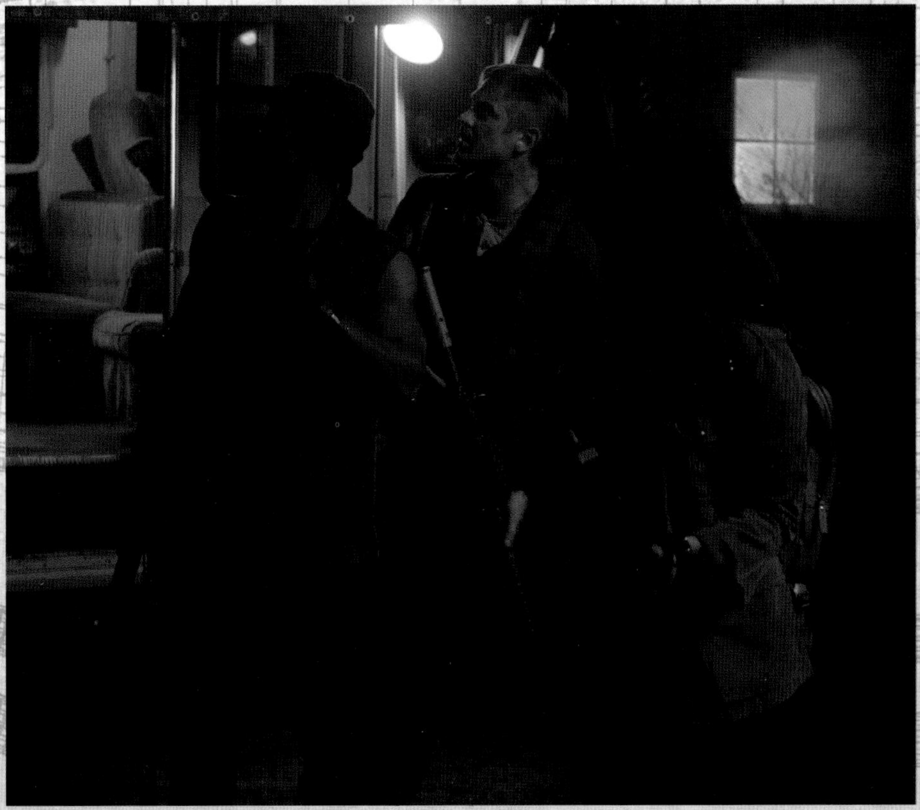

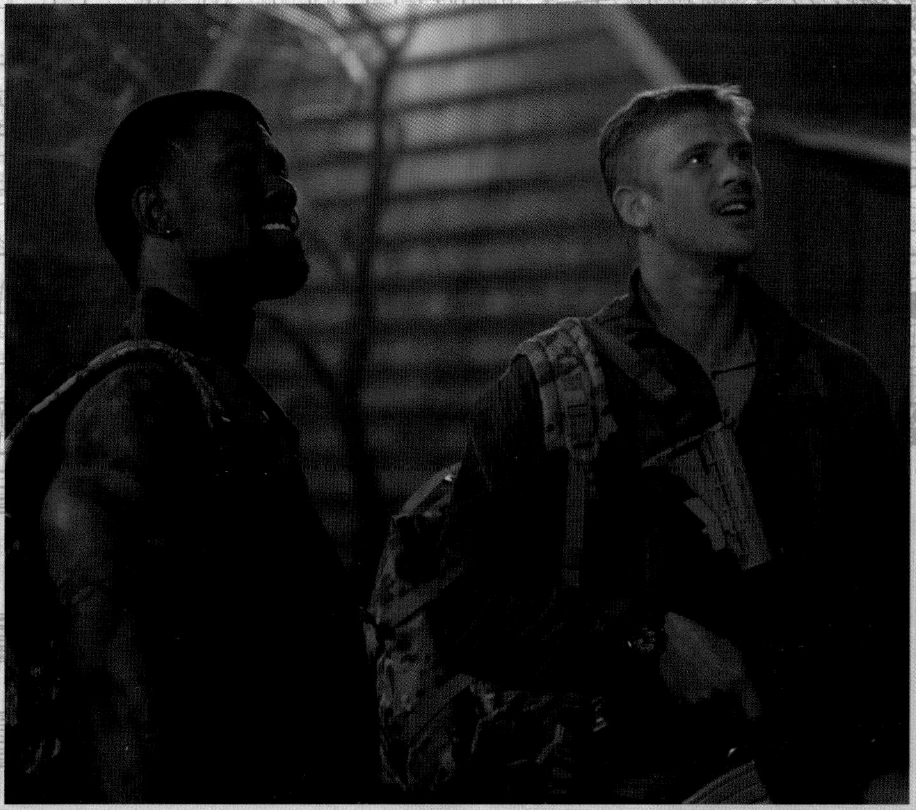

THE SHIP APPEARS

Deep in a forest in rural Georgia, Traeger arrives at the Fugitive Predator's ship crash site with Rory. The area is cordoned off with electrified fencing and heavily guarded by Stargazer's mercenaries. Stadium floodlights illuminate an eerie sight: a trail of plowed trees and pulped debris gouged through the forest, leading to the downed spacecraft. Soldiers secure tarps over the ship and tech guys roll in a giant screen trailing cables.

From a hilltop, McKenna monitors the situation, rifle locked and loaded. He watches as Traeger leads Rory up to the ship's hatch. The boy punches in a code and the door opens.

"The spaceship was hard because there's no right or wrong spaceship," says Hamish Purdy. "We don't have anything to check up against. We decided this spaceship has to match our character. We knew that it had to look like it was his ship, not just a ship he acquired. So we just keyed off on certain little textures on his body and introduced those so you could feel that it came from the Predator planet."

"It had to be Predator intelligence in a mechanical form," says Martin Whist. "That applies to everything. It applies to the console in the ship, the design of the interior, the design of the exterior. Everything Predator. We wanted to pull it away from that tribal design and make it this organic but intelligent tech-look."

RIGHT: Early concept art of the Fugitive Predator's ship, covered in tarps and surrounded by Traeger's men.

Unlike the Fugitive Predator ship's interior, the exterior was created mostly through visual effects. "That's the thing about movie-making now with blue screens," says Purdy. "There's an enormous spaceship, but we're actually just building the lip of the spaceship so that they can climb into it. We still have to get into sets, still have to get them the right positioning and get lit, but there's a little bit of a disconnect there. We did build a bit of a rooftop set piece so that they could fight on it, but the rest of it will be CG."

ABOVE AND ABOVE RIGHT: Concepts for the Fugitive Predator's ship being transported.

RIGHT: Filming location of the Fugitive Predator ship's crash site.

BELOW: The mouth of the ramp door was the only section of the Fugitive Predator ship's exterior constructed practically. The rest of the ship was added in VFX.

"THE QUARRY'S A GREAT SETTING, VERY DRAMATIC. IT WAS A PERFECT SETTING FOR WHAT WE WANTED TO DO."

John Starke, Executive Producer

THE PREDATOR: THE ART AND MAKING OF THE FILM

THIS PAGE: Top left: night shoot at the Pitt River Quarries in British Columbia; top right: Sterling K Brown and Jacob Tremblay on location at the quarry; bottom left and right: Sterling K Brown, Jacob Tremblay, and Niall Matter enter the Ark.

"OUR ASSASSIN PREDATOR IS 11FT TALL, AND IT'S ACTUALLY HIS SHIP. THE FUGITIVE PREDATOR, HE'S 7FT TALL, SO EVEN HE IS SMALL IN THIS SHIP."

Hamish Purdy, Set Decorator

ABOARD THE SHIP

A brilliantly constructed set, the interior of the Fugitive Predator's ship is huge. This is the Predators' space, and you can feel it.

"Our Assassin Predator, which is a CG character, is 11ft tall and it's actually his ship," says Hamish Purdy. "So it's built for an 11-ft-tall character, which is why the rear console completely blocks human actors when you're looking at it from below. The Fugitive Predator, he's 7ft tall, so even he is small in this ship. And then you have Rory, and he's minuscule in a ship like that."

"The steps were just a few inches taller than other steps," remembers Augusto Aguilera. "Everything, the doorways, the console, the buttons, everything was oversized. The production of this thing is crazy. The minds that go into building that thing are amazing."

"We had to stay on top of the scale of the rooms when we worked on them," says Purdy regarding the proportions of the craft's interior features. "We'd use cardboard cutouts, silhouettes of the Assassin, and stand them in there so we'd understand, 'Oh, his keypad has to be here, not here, obviously.' You don't want to miss things like the scale of steps being for his scale, not human scale. Installing things, I had to understand that his hands are 20 inches long, so everything is different."

A crucial aspect of designing the ship was ensuring that filming inside it would be as easy as possible. "You get into the idea of how do you float around that set and acquire the coverage you need to allow scenes to play out," says Bill Bannerman. "How can you bring in a techno-crane? How can you bring in a 75-ft-long telescopic arm? How do you figure out the physics of a fulcrum and a pivot point where you can sit on one place on that set and be able to reach everywhere? What happens if you decide it has to be here, but here is a solid wall? Well, we've got to make the wall wild so we can pull it out and stick in a camera crane, or stick in a light, or stick in some form of technology that we need in order to do our job."

Integrating LED lighting into the set itself lent the filmmakers freedom and control. "They're so small that we can fit them into fissures and under counters and inside equipment, and it really brings the sets to life," explains Purdy. "It was important for the Predator ship to test some red. We associate red lighting with the Predator from the very first countdown; we saw it on his wrist in '87. And so we introduced that into the set and we found that running that LED lighting at about 3–5% of its full brightness was the most effective. When it was its dimmest and its most subtle glow, still very important to have it there.

"One of the companies we bought a lot of LEDs from, we bought all the red LED they had in North America. When you've figured out what works, all of a sudden you need all of it. We bought spools and spools of it. It was throughout the ship. It's in all the fissures and throughout the floor, entire consoles all wrapped in LEDs. It's early days yet because it's still labor intensive, and it's not easily salvageable when the set is done. But DPs love it, it's super controllable and repeatable, and it's definitely the way we're going to do a lot of sets from here on."

RIGHT: "Red was an important color in the original *Predator* with the laser, and so we latched onto that in the Fugitive Predator ship. LEDs are a new technology and they respond differently to the camera, and sometimes they flicker because of different frame rates. We found the reds were sometimes too much for the camera's chip to hold. We had to control the intensity and adjust our LUTs (Look-Up Tables are used to modify the original image into the display image when color grading) in post-production so we could capture certain reds without streaking or tearing or blowing out, which we found a lot of LEDs did." Larry Fong, Director of Photography

"EVERYTHING, THE DOORWAYS, THE CONSOLE, THE BUTTONS, EVERYTHING WAS OVERSIZED. THE PRODUCTION OF THIS THING IS CRAZY."

Augusto Aguilera (Nettles)

"AT ANY ONE TIME IT WAS PROBABLY GETTING CLOSE TO ABOUT 100 WEAPONS IN TOTAL, AND VARIOUS MODELS AND SIZES AND CALIBERS."

Rob Fournier, Lead Armorer

THE BATTLE

As the Loonies create a diversion on the perimeter of the site, McKenna sneaks in unseen with the aid of the Fugitive Predator's cloaking sphere and gets onto the ship to rescue Rory. Taking Traeger hostage, he leads him back outside to negotiate their escape. Traeger plays hardball, but the stand-off is brought to a premature close by the arrival of the Assassin Predator, who cuts a bloody swath through Loony and mercenary alike.

"That is a fairly complicated gunfight, as far as choreography goes," says Alex Burdett. "Every character is involved, so there's lots of coverage. It's a fast-paced scene. It wasn't that any one thing was daunting, it was just a very long laundry list of gags every day."

Burdett explains the responsibilities he and his team take on during production. "We deal with the explosions. If you look in the background, we have to keep the fires going as if the explosion just happened. That burning aftermath sometimes can go on for days afterwards. We deal with rigging our cars and the jeeps to roll and blow up. There were a lot of practical effects. Lots of Predator cannon hits. Lots of gunfire. Practically wrecking jeeps and SUVs, that sort of thing. Lots of carnage."

"Planning, it's all about planning," says John Starke. "The crews are just fabulous. We have a great special-effects team. We have great technicians. I mean, all of the lighting was pre-rigged and set in place days before shooting. We scouted the location probably five times. We have a model of the woods that we rehearse with. We've blocked all of the action here so that when we do come to shooting, our work is as efficient as possible."

With the Assassin Predator being computer-generated, his scenes involve a high level of collaboration between different production departments. "Basically, on every shot we consult with the VFX guys for what we need to provide in terms of the proxy for the CG characters," says Burdett. "How it's moving, whether it's going to be on fire, or if it's smashing something or throwing someone. The Assassin Predator has quite an arsenal of weapons on him too, so we have to know what he's using in each shot. Shot by shot we're keeping track of whether he's using a blade or a cannon or a laser. One of the VFX guys is always there for us to deal with, someone like Matt Sloan."

LEFT: Our heroes enter the fray. Top: Thomas Jane and Keegan-Michael Key; center: Trevante Rhodes, Olivia Munn, and Augusto Aguilera; bottom: Boyd Holbrook and Jacob Tremblay.

"Because we have a couple of full CG characters and a lot of effects, like the laser blasts and explosions, it's just keeping an eye on the shooting crew and making sure they're getting exactly what we need," confirms Sloan. "The Assassin Predator is 11ft tall, so making sure the cameras are framed properly for him, that we have tracking information, LIDAR information, color information that will go to our vendors so they'll be able to integrate the big guy into the plates—generally just helping out and making sure that the shooting crew have the support they need from visual effects."

With almost every member of the cast taking up arms in the battle, it was a challenging sequence for lead armorer Rob Fournier. "At any one time, it was probably getting close to about a hundred weapons in total, and various models and sizes and calibers."

Such extensive weapons work required preparation with the actors. "We spent about three weeks training our lead cast on the basic firearms, and they all got really efficient at it over time," says Fournier.

With each different character having their own weapons of choice, Fournier explains the process of selection. "Actually, the firearms were picked by Shane Black himself. The decisions were character driven, so every single firearm is different. We had to spend time with each actor in order to become proficient with their firearm, whether it was a pistol or a rifle.

"Boyd has a standard M4, but it's an extended barrel version. Shane wanted something a little different for him, because his character was a soldier and would have a big knowledge of firearms. So, we

ABOVE: "Honestly? This *Predator* is far more bad-ass than the other *Predators*. We've got more guns, more fights, more explosions. And we stay true to the original *Predator*, which is really great." Augusto Aguilera

RIGHT: When the Assassin Predator wades into the battle, everybody dives for cover.

gave him a two-tone M4, and he also has two sidearms: a .45 caliber sidearm on his right hip, and on his left hip a 9mm.

"With Olivia, she learned very quickly how to handle firearms. She only really had to be trained on one, but she wanted to be cross trained, so we spent a little bit of time with different weapons for her. She had to look good, but not too good, because of her scientific background. She wasn't a soldier, but she had to look like she was proficient, like she knew the basics of gun handling."

Fournier reveals the most difficult aspect wasn't teaching the cast about the weapons at all. "Tracking down the actors in between shots to make sure that I get the firearms back, that's probably one of the biggest challenges. We have a large cast, we have a big location, and a lot of night shooting—just keeping track of where everyone is and keeping stock of the firearms can get a little taxing."

There are also safety concerns with so much weapons work and practical effects being executed around the principal cast. "We do sparks, a lot of different types of sparks," says Burdett, talking about the pyrotechnic effects used when filming gunfights. "Which one we use depends on how close they are going to be to the cast, so we will go with the smaller one if it's going to be very close. They're directional, so we can point them away from the actors, but we don't really get into the heavier sparks stuff with the principals. Having said that, we did use large air cannons with Boyd. They were some decent-sized sparks."

THE HUNT

The battle comes to an abrupt end when the Assassin Predator enters the ship and closes the door. With Stargazer and the Loonies still squabbling outside, the Assassin Predator speaks through the spacecraft's loudspeaker, informing them that the hunt is about to begin. Granted a five-minute head-start, the humans reluctantly band together and arm themselves as best they can for their flight though the woods.

Having stowed some Predator weapons from Stargazer when he left, Traeger straps on an alien shoulder cannon, fixing its firing sensor to his neck. One of his mercenaries selects the shuriken, not realizing it returns to the thrower like a boomerang. When he deploys it against their Predator pursuer, he realizes too late that he has no way of safely catching it, and costs himself a perfectly good hand. Wounded and cornered by the Assassin Predator, he pleads that he is unarmed and poses no threat. But the new Predator only has so much respect for the old rules, and rips his spine out through his mouth.

"The thing we all love about the Predator of the original films is there was a code of honor," says John Davis. "A hunter hunts, but

there are rules and there's a way it's done. But as the Predator is upgrading, its society is changing its goals, and this metamorphosis is changing the order of things."

"I think the most exciting part of the movie is the hunt," says Matt Sloan. "It's your classic Predator hunt. The creature has lured the humans into the forest and he hunts them down one by one. It's pretty simple, but it's just such classic Predator that you can't help but have fun. All the fan-favorite weapons are still there, but, like the Predator himself, some of them have been upgraded. Some of them do new things. But the shoulder cannons and the gauntlet, they're still there, and then there's a few surprises as well."

Baxley and Coyle volunteer to distract the Assassin Predator to give the others time to flee and set a trap for the creature. Not easily fooled, however, the Assassin Predator starts racking up the body count. "The movie has the same sort of feel as the 80s action pictures," says Matt Sloan. "It doesn't try and get too philosophical. It's fast, it's a rollercoaster, and it gets to the action early and just keeps the pace up throughout the entire film while letting you grow attached to these characters, who all then die brutally."

THIS PAGE: Clockwise from top left: Augusto Aguilera as Nettles; Olivia Munn as Casey; Boyd Holbrook as McKenna; Trevante Rhodes as Nebraska Williams. "The group dynamic is as you see on the film. Everyone's pretty confident in who they are and who their character is. They know how to jump into the space and handle business. Bounding off of each other is always a fun thing. Whenever you have people who are good at their job, it's just fun." Trevante Rhodes

As the Loonies set off claymores and phosphorous around the Assassin Predator, absolute mayhem reigns. Traeger, free-firing with the shoulder cannon, doesn't notice his pants setting alight. When Casey shouts to warn him, Traeger turns suddenly to look at her and realizes too late that he has triggered the neck sensor to fire the cannon, blowing his own head off.

"Traeger didn't see it coming at all," laughs Sterling K. Brown. "It definitely does add to the frantic, comedic pace that happens within the course of the movie because, in the midst of all hell braking loose, the audience gets this moment of like, 'Yeah!' Because they're not necessarily rooting for Traeger, if I did my job right, and that's okay."

LEFT: "The blending of action and horror is a testament to Shane as a creative person. You take this world that is innately incredibly scary, and then you bring in this person who has an amazing texture of action and comedy and heart. It's just a cool amalgamation of things." Trevante Rhodes

ABOVE: Night shooting in the British Columbia woods.

RIGHT: Concept art for Traeger's Mobile Command Center.

ON THE RUN

axley spots an opportunity to strike the wounded Assassin Predator and charges up a fallen tree trunk, leaping on top of the creature and burying his knife in its eye. Alight from the phosphorous, Baxley is thrown through the air by the Assassin Predator and is impaled on a jutting branch 20ft overhead.

Everyone pulls together to bring off these set pieces. "Special effects did a plant-on for the impalement," says Alex Burdett. "Make-up effects provide the gore, and stunts do the rigging. It's a remote location, so logistically it's challenging. There's quite a bit of fire, and interaction with a CG character on fire. So we built a steel proxy to create a lighting effect for the VFX guys, and we also had interactive LED suits. The lighting department built them so stunt performers can wear them to interact with the actors. It's a group effort."

"It's a joint effort between all departments," confirms Martin Whist. "Visual effects, practical special effects, and lighting. A lot of the effects that will be put in, like a gun blast coming from the digital Assassin character, need to have interactive lighting, like when an explosion occurs. Interactive lighting is a hard visual effect to achieve, so that would be done practically. Everything needs to be choreographed with special effects, and with stunts as well, for any kind of practical action where humans might be injured or affected by the Assassin Predator. It becomes a very, very complicated dance between the camera, lighting, visual effects, practical effects, and my oversight of how the ground needs to lay out to help facilitate it all.

"My role is primarily at the beginning, to lay the stage in such a way that it conforms to the action. So I will go out and look at the location, I will talk to Shane and find out what his requirements are, what he wants out of it, and then I'll make a pitch to the other departments in terms of the action: a guy up here, an explosion there, here someone will get yanked, there'll be a guy up in the tree there. Once everything has been communally agreed upon, then everybody will start working on their contributions and we'll all co-ordinate and adjust to the visual effects. The whole scene morphs into what it ultimately becomes, what ends up on camera. It's an interesting collaborative process when dealing with unknowns like the digital Predator character."

BELOW: Traeger (Sterling K Brown) being pursued by the Assassin Predator in the woods.

RIGHT: Coyle (Keegan-Michael Key) has a long, hard look inside himself.

FAR RIGHT: Williams (Trevante Rhodes) gives Rory (Jacob Tremblay) a lift.

ABOVE AND LEFT: The Loonies and Stargazer are forced together as they are all quarry in the Assassin Predator's hunt.

RIGHT: On location in the woods near Langley, British Columbia.

Wounded and on the back foot, the Assassin Predator strikes out and disembowels Coyle, leaving him slumped against a tree staring at his own guts in his lap. "It's probably the most grisly death in the movie," says Keegan-Michael Key. "Rule of thumb, if you're gonna die, have the best death."

McKenna and the surviving Loonies run through the forest, making for the chopper and a way out of the killing field. Overtaking them in the trees, the injured Assassin Predator takes the helicopter out and attacks. His prime target is Rory, having decided that his facility with mathematics and languages presents a potential upgrade opportunity. Swatting aside McKenna and Casey, he picks up the boy and bounds off into the woods.

RAGING WARRIORS

Accompanied by Williams and Nettles, McKenna pursues the Assassin Predator to a quarry, where it has hidden its own cloaked spacecraft. With Rory trapped in a pod onboard and the creature firing up the engines, McKenna and the others leap off the side of the quarry onto the top of the ship.

"A bunch of our characters actually end up standing on top of the Predator's spaceship as it is lifting off and beginning to move off, trying to leave the atmosphere," says Matt Sloan. "So it's the trick of having them having to figure out very quickly how to get out of the situation and disable the ship so that McKenna can get his son back. That bit's a literal rollercoaster."

"Originally, we were going to cheat the Assassin's spaceship," says Martin Whist. "The Fugitive Predator's ship was going to play for both ships. But now it's a real thing, fully designed. It's smaller and sleeker than the Fugitive Predator's ship, more of an attack ship."

"For the spaceship, we built a deck and staged it on a large gimbal," says Alex Burdett. "We had the cast standing on it and hit them with gusts of wind."

RIGHT: Early concept art for the crashed Predator ship scene, by Warren Flanagan.

When the Assassin Predator activates the ship's force field, McKenna falls flat on the hull, Williams leaps up in the air, and Nettles does nothing. "Only one person makes the right choice and it isn't me," laughs Augusto Aguilera. "I don't make any choice at all. I just stand there and die. I get my legs cut off by a force field and then I fall to my death." He considers this. "Or maybe I don't die. I don't know. Who knows? Maybe there's a spin-off of my character, which would be the weirdest spin-off."

McKenna and Williams are left face-to-face, one below the force field and one on top of it. Unable to hold on, Williams too falls to his death. Sliding off the top of the ship, McKenna rides the inside of the force field underneath the ship.

"We utilized fiber glass to be the force field," says Jonathan Rothbart, "but to support the guys jumping around on top of it, it had to be pretty thick, so we ran into all sorts of reflection problems. When there's two guys either side looking at each other, you can't really shoot it through the glass because of the reflections. So we went through it step by step, and each shot needed its own approach in how to achieve the effect. No one gag was going to get it done."

Briefly gaining access to the ship, McKenna manages to do enough damage to disable it before he is forced out of a hatch by the Assassin Predator. Dragged through the treeline, he ends up falling through the boughs and hanging upside down, barely conscious, as the spacecraft crashes into the Okefenokee Swamp in Georgia. Casey has followed them on a motorcycle, and even their old friend the Predator hound has tracked them down. There in the swamp, McKenna and Casey stage their final battle with the Assassin Predator.

"You don't want it to look like the backyard of a baseball field in the sandlot," says Bill Bannerman. "It's about production value. We had to do it in two levels so we could add a very grandiose set, because the ceiling clearances in the Mammoth Studios stages only go up to about 35ft before you have to deal with lighting and grips and electrics, and our set needed to be about 60ft tall."

"Building the swamp was quite a challenge because the stage was not tall enough to do the whole thing," confirms Martin Whist. "I had to do it in two parts, build the upper swamp at the top of a cliff and where all the action takes place, and then overlap that to match on another stage the lower area, which was the water and the base of the cliff. We had to split it in two.

"The stage was massive, but it's only 40ft to the perms. If you have a 30ft tree and then a cliff which needs to be higher than the Assassin, who's 10ft tall, then you're already well over the stage

height. We talked about doing it outside, but in the end this was the best technique."

"We used Styrofoam, trying to replicate a certain type of rock texture," says Hamish Purdy. "Styrofoam is very useful, and it's very fast. You can get it in, get it glued together and start painting it right away. For the swamp itself we brought in a lot of road crush to create the topography before we started building cliff faces. There's actually a lot of real dirt and rocks and plants in that set."

THIS PAGE: Shane Black and Boyd Holbrook on location for the final showdown.

NEXT PAGE: Concept art by Warren Flanagan of the crash site where the final battle occurs.

THE PREDATOR: THE ART AND MAKING OF THE FILM

"There's a lot of real stuff on the swamp sets," says Jesse Joslin. "The trees are all real. A lot of the ground fill is also real. So there was a lot of machinery having to come in and out and it became a bit of a problem during the day with the trucks dropping the road crush and stuff to start sculpting the set. We were mostly able to steer clear of night shifts, but those poor guys had to switch to nights for a good month and a half to get that bulked in."

"The most exciting thing about the film is the way all kinds of genre elements blended together into this stew," says Shane Black, summing up the movie. "It isn't just one more story about the Predator; it encompasses everything about the Predator through the genre, has all the different things you want to see packed into one film. I'm lucky, truly blessed, to be afforded this opportunity, to still be on the map after 30 years and still be operating at this level where the budget is this big, the stars are this good, and I've been given this much latitude to play in the *Predator* sandbox. Pinch me, because I must be sleeping. This is going to be a hoot of a movie. I know we can cut a hell of a trailer."

"THERE'S A LOT OF REAL
STUFF ON THE SWAMP
SETS. THE TREES ARE
ALL REAL, A LOT OF THE
GROUND FILL IS ALSO REAL."

Jesse Joslin, Construction Coordinator

THIS PAGE: The sets at Mammoth Studios were
painstakingly constructed to match the locations in British
Columbia, and both were dressed to look like the Okefenokee
swamp on the Georgia-Florida line.

ACKNOWLEDGMENTS

All books are the fruit of collaboration, but the author would like to extend particular thanks to: Andy Jones, Natasha MacKenzie, and Simon Ward at Titan Books for their work and guidance; Nicole Spiegel at Fox, problem-solver extraordinaire; Tom Woodruff Jr, Alec Gillis, and Mike Heintzelman at Amalgamated Dynamics Inc, who were so helpful in providing their artwork; Alex Burdett, Trevor Addie, and Martin Whist, who were generous with their time and recollections. Finally, thank you to Shane Black.